Operation:
TECTONIC
FURY
Unlocking Earth's Geologic Mysteries

NATIONAL GEOGRAPHIC

The
JASON
Project

A nonprofit subsidiary of the National Geographic Society, The JASON Project connects students with great explorers and great events to inspire and motivate them to learn science. JASON works with the National Geographic Society, the National Oceanic and Atmospheric Administration (NOAA), the National Aeronautics and Space Administration (NASA), the U.S. Department of Energy, the Smithsonian Institution, and other leading organizations to develop multimedia science curricula based on their cutting-edge missions of exploration and discovery. By providing educators with those same inspirational experiences—and giving them the tools and resources to improve science teaching— JASON seeks to reenergize them for a lasting, positive impact on students.

Visit *www.jason.org* to learn more about The JASON Project, or email us at *info@jason.org*.

Cover Design: Ryan Kincade, The JASON Project

Cover Images

Main cover and title page: G. Brad Lewis Photography.

Front cover thumbnails: Peter Haydock, The JASON Project.

Back cover thumbnails: (top left) Student Argonaut Connor Bebb. Photo by Bill Jewell, The JASON Project; (middle right) Student Argonaut Emily Judah. Photo by Bill Jewell, The JASON Project; (bottom left) Teacher Argonaut Cindy Duguay. Photo by Bill Jewell, The JASON Project; (bottom right) Halong Bay, Vietnam. Photo by Arianos/Wikimedia Commons; Volcano. Photo by David Karnå/Wikimedia Commons.

Published by The JASON Project.

Requests for permission to copy or distribute any part of this work should be addressed to

The JASON Project
Permissions Requests
44983 Knoll Square
Ashburn, VA 20147

Phone: 888-527-6600
Fax: 877-370-8988

ISBN 978-1-935211-36-5

Printed in the United States of America
by the Courier Companies, Inc.

10 9 8 7 6 5 4 3

Contents

Operation:
TECTONIC FURY

Paul Zahl/National Geographic Image Collection

Getting Started with *Operation: Tectonic Fury*

Developed in collaboration with our partners at National Geographic, NOAA, the U.S. Department of Energy, the Smithsonian Institution, and other leading organizations, *Operation: Tectonic Fury* is built on a Mission framework to capture the energy and excitement of authentic exploration and discovery. The *Operation* consists of four captivating Missions that provide the real-world challenges, the scientific background knowledge, and the tools to help you solve each Mission challenge.

Let's take a closer look at the parts of each Mission!

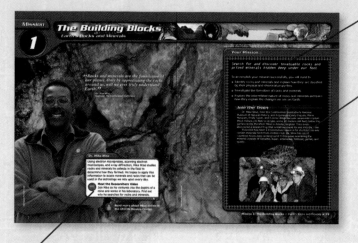

Mission Objectives

Each Mission starts with a list of objectives that you will find on this opening page.

Join The Team

Your Mission begins with an invitation to the join the Host Researcher and Argonaut team. You will work side-by-side with this team as they guide you through your study of geology.

Video and Online Resources

You will also see icons directing you to the Host Researcher Video, where you will get to know more about the Mission team leader. Watch for these icons and others. They indicate when you will find multimedia resources online in the **JASON Mission Center.**

Introduction Article

Once you have your objectives and have met the team, each new Mission will introduce you to a day in the life of the Host Researcher and the unique work that brings this scientist face-to-face with geology concepts.

Mission Briefing Video

See these adventures come alive in every Mission Briefing Video, which gives an action-packed introduction to the Mission objectives and key science concepts.

Mission Briefing Articles

Gather all of your background information and clues through a series of Mission Briefing Articles that guide you through the science of geology, so that you can complete your Mission objectives.

Full-color graphics enhance the description and explanation of essential science concepts, so you can clearly see the ideas presented in the briefings.

Fast Facts and Examples

You will find interesting things you have never thought of before in Fast Facts and Examples.

Researcher Tools

Check out the amazing tools that researchers use during their explorations in the field. From CT scanners to satellites, you will learn how these tools help researchers unlock the secrets of our planet.

Explorer's Connections

Check out examples of Dr. Bob Ballard's research around the world.

Team Highlights

Get an up-close view of the investigations that our Host Researchers and Argonauts conducted during their field work for *Operation: Tectonic Fury*.

Mission Labs

Put your knowledge to work with several hands-on labs in each Mission. The labs provide opportunities to practice and refine the skills you need in order to complete your mission objectives. In these labs, you will build tools, conduct investigations, collect data, and describe your observations and conclusions in your JASON Journal.

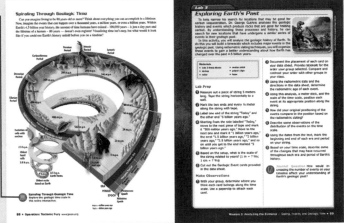

Additional Online Resources

You will also find other great resources in the **JASON Mission Center**, including your JASON Journal. Use it to record your work and experiences as you complete your *Operation: Tectonic Fury* Missions. Check the JASON site often for live events and Webcasts that will provide updates on your Mission and on other breaking news in science.

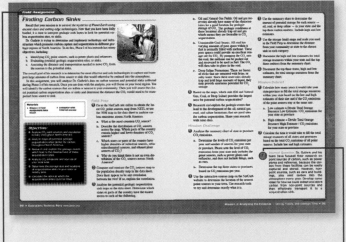

Connections

Learn to look for and find the amazing connections between science concepts and other things that you experience in the world around you. *Connections* highlight thought-provoking links that you can explore between science and human culture, history, geography, math, literature, strange phenomena, and other interesting topics.

Field Assignment

Field Assignments at the conclusion of each Mission give you the opportunity to put your new science skills and ideas to work in the field. To complete your Mission, you will need to accomplish the objectives set out in a Mission Challenge, and then provide an analysis during your Mission Debrief.

Argonaut Videos, Journals, and Photo Galleries

Join the Argo team as they conduct their field work for selected Missions around the country. Log into the **JASON Mission Center** to read the Argonaut journals and take a look at the photo galleries documenting their field experiences!

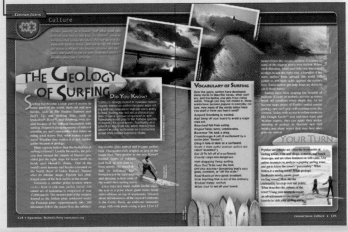

Your Tour of the JASON Mission Center

The **JASON Mission Center** is your online hub for *Operation: Tectonic Fury* content and resources and for the Argonaut community. Your JASON experience will come to life through interactive games, digital labs, video segments, your own JASON Journals, and other community resources and tools that support the Missions in this book.

Create Your Own Free Student Account

If your teacher has made an account for you, simply log into the **JASON Mission Center.** Otherwise, follow these simple steps below to create your own account.

1. Go to *www.jason.org*.
2. Look for the **JASON Mission Center** in the upper right corner.
3. Click **Register**.
4. Choose "Student" as your role –OR– if your teacher provided you with a classroom code, click the link to enter it now.
5. Enter a username and select a password for your account that you can easily remember.

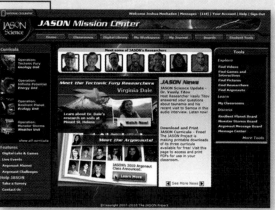

The JASON Mission Center *Home Page*

Welcome to your **JASON Mission Center** home page. From here you can quickly access all the wonderful JASON tools and resources as you begin your mission. Take a moment to read the latest JASON news, try a search of the Digital Library, or jump right into *Operation: Tectonic Fury* on the Web!

Here are some of the things you will see . . .

Your Resources and Tools

Powerful online tools are always at your fingertips. Use the *Digital Library* to find any JASON resource quickly and easily. Save and organize your favorites in *My Workspace*. View assignments and community updates in your *Classrooms* menu. These resources and more are always accessible through the *Tools* menu at the top of the **JASON Mission Center** page.

My Journals and Other Community Tools

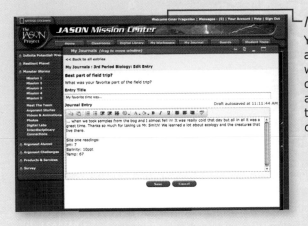

Your student account in the **JASON Mission Center** includes an online JASON Journal that allows you to take notes, write about what you have learned, and respond to journal questions during the Missions. Other Community Tools include a moderated message board, classroom home pages, and tools to communicate with JASON researchers about their ongoing work in the field.

Online Version of Operation: Tectonic Fury

This entire student edition book is also available to you online, for easy access anytime, anywhere. You can view any page from any Mission.

Team Info, Videos, and Photo Galleries

Learn more about the Host Researchers and the Argonauts from their biographies and journals. Video segments feature the Mission teams in action. Photo galleries provide additional views of the researchers and Argonauts at work, as well as stunning collections of more geology concepts in our world.

Peter Haydock/The JASON Project

Peter Haydock/The JASON Project

Interactive Games

Visit the JASON Mission Center for digital labs and games. See if you can recreate some of the world's most amazing landforms using your understanding of geologic processes or explore mines to determine the identities of mystery minerals.

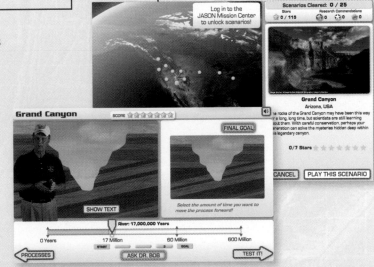

Live Events

Communicate with great explorers through great events. JASON researchers work on the cutting-edge of science and are eager to share their stories of discovery and inspiration with students around the world.

Your Mission begins at *www.jason.org*

Operation: TECTONIC FURY

Operation Overview

Welcome to *Operation: Tectonic Fury* where our mission is to figure out how our planet works and how it has changed over the past several billion years.

Much of what we know about Earth has changed since I was in school. I was taught that the largest mountain range on the planet was the Himalayas, and that there was little life in the deepest parts of the ocean due to the absence of sunlight. Scientists also did not know how old the ocean floor was, nor did they believe the continents were moving. But now, things are different. Clues to the true history of Earth were hidden deep on the ocean floor. To unravel the mystery of our Earth, we had to travel to the bottom of the ocean!

Discovery

As a young child, I was always fascinated by the ocean. Stories of Captain Nemo from *20,000 Leagues Under the Sea* inspired me to learn more about our planet and quite literally go where no one has gone before. After studying chemistry and geology in college, I became a marine geologist.

In the summer of 1977, a small group of scientists, including myself, crammed into a tiny submarine to explore a region of the ocean floor where the very crust of the planet was moving apart and new earth was actually being created. Our mission was to examine a segment of a giant undersea mountain range near the Galápagos Islands. We did not know what to expect, but what we discovered changed some of the ways we view our planet.

We were shocked to find a tremendous diversity of life, including six-foot tube worms and enormous clam shells filled with slimy organisms. These organisms were able to survive in complete darkness and extreme heat, and under tremendous pressure. Two years later, on another segment of this underwater mountain range near Mexico, we witnessed giant, chimney-like vents ejecting pure gold, silver, copper, and zinc at temperatures that melted our lead thermometers.

Our discoveries were groundbreaking, but they were just a few of many that help us better understand our planet. Today, we are still challenged by many questions. What makes up Earth? How does it work?

Dr. Robert D. Ballard
Founder and Chief Scientist
The JASON Project

Operation Overview Video
Join Dr. Ballard on a journey to discover the mysteries of our planet.

What is Geology?

Earth has been continually changing throughout its 4.5 billion year history. **Geology** is the study of Earth and its history as recorded in rocks. The word geology comes from the Greek *geo*, which means "Earth," and *logy*, which means "study of."

To study geology, one must have a keen eye for detail and strong detective skills to analyze geologic evidence collected from different areas around the world. The data geologists gather helps them create hypotheses that link what may have happened thousands—even millions—of years ago to the landforms and events we see today.

Geology and the World Around Us

Geology is all around us, and it affects every aspect of our lives. The schools you learn in, the houses you live in, and the technology you rely upon every day depend on our understanding of geology.

For instance, your computer is made up of minerals that are mined from geologic deposits. Glass cups, reading glasses, and mirrors are made from silica found in beach sand. The water you drink is pumped up from wells where water is stored underground or stored in reservoirs that collect river water flowing from mountains.

The availability of minerals and the topography of the land determine the life an area can support. The life that thrives on Earth today depends upon geology for survival, as it is the foundation for every living organism on this planet.

But, just as Earth provides the resources we need to live, it can also destroy life and property. Throughout history, people have suffered great losses from powerful geologic events, like earthquakes, volcanoes, and tsunamis. While we cannot prevent these disasters, the study of geology can help us reduce the devastation these geologic events can cause.

Your Missions

To help you explore the mysteries behind this planet, you will join a top notch team of scientists. The JASON Host Researchers, along with the JASON Argonauts, will take you on four missions and provide you with the necessary tools to help you unlock some of the geologic mysteries stored in this dynamic ever-changing planet.

In Mission 1, Dr. Mike Wise will introduce you to the building blocks upon which geology is based—rocks and minerals.

Building upon the basics of geology, Dr. Virginia Dale will explore weathering and erosion in Mission 2. You will see how these processes affect Earth's changing face, and form the soil that supports life on Earth.

In Mission 3, you will journey through geologic time with Dr. George Guthrie. Using fossils and technology, you will learn how scientists have constructed the story behind Earth's long history.

Finally, in Mission 4, you will venture deep into Earth's interior with Dr. Walter Smith. Here, you will learn about some of the processes that have been, and still are, changing our planet every day. This mission will give you a better understanding as to why continents move, earthquakes occur, and volcanoes erupt.

Challenges

Society faces a number of global challenges today, including food shortages, global warming, loss of natural habitat, and a need for a reliable and safe energy supply. The study of geology can help us address these challenges. As new technologies are developed, and as young scientists like you become inspired to explore and discover the mysteries locked within Earth, we will gain new insights into the natural processes of our planet. These discoveries will help provide solutions today, as well as prepare us for a sustainable future.

We have made remarkable discoveries about how our planet works and how it has changed over the past several billion years. However, we still have much to discover! When I go out on scientific expeditions, I always keep in mind that my greatest discovery is the one I haven't made yet. What will your greatest discovery be?

Good luck, Argo!

Mapping

What Is a Map?

What tool can you think of that can be used to represent our planet's wealth of natural and human-made resources on a simple piece of paper? A map!

Maps have been used for centuries, helping people explore and better understand their surroundings. Designed to provide specific information, they give users a visual representation of a location or an area.

Reference maps represent key features of the land, such as the borders of countries, cities, and towns. For example, these maps can help guide people along park trails or through city streets.

Other maps are designed to represent certain themes, summarizing information that represent patterns. Thematic maps might provide data about the distribution of rock and mineral deposits, human population density throughout the world, the average rainfall of a region, or the location and distribution of soil types.

Throughout *Operation: Tectonic Fury*, you will use these types of maps just as geologists do. In Mission 1, you will use maps similar to the ones Dr. Mike Wise uses to locate precious rocks and minerals. In Mission 2, you will explore a variety of thematic maps that help us determine the best crops to grow in different parts of the world with Dr. Virginia Dale. Maps will also be helpful in Mission 3 when you scour the planet with Dr. George Guthrie looking for suitable locations to store greenhouse gases. In Mission 4, you will work with maps developed by Dr. Walter Smith to locate earthquakes, volcanoes, and underwater seamounts.

The Argonauts meet Dr. Walter Smith at the Oregon Museum of Science and Industry. Here, they project the maps Walter has made using information gained from satellites onto NOAA's Science On a Sphere® globe. The biggest discovery they make is that most of the ocean has not been mapped.

Peter Haydock/The JASON Project

Math Connection

1. **Locate your city, or closest city, on a world map.**

2. **Now, choose a place in the world where you would like to visit.**

3. **Measure the distance between your city and your destination. For globes, it might be easier to measure the distance with the help of a string.**

4. **Using the scale on your map, calculate the actual distance.**

Mapping Technology

Maps have come a long way since they were first developed. Recent advances in technology have increased our capability to explore regions of the world that were once too difficult or dangerous to explore!

Global Positioning System (GPS) technology uses satellite information to pinpoint your location anywhere on the planet. It can give drivers directions to where they want to go, and provide real-time elevation measurements, and longitude and latitude coordinates anywhere in the world. A number of GPS satellites are in orbit, making it a popular tool for land, sea, and air navigation, as well as map making and land surveying.

Satellites are also used to help map the ocean floor as well as other dangerous and inaccessible areas on land. Mapping satellites carry specialized equipment, such as radar, cameras, and other imagers, to collect information that can be used to make maps.

Geographic Information Systems (GIS) is another technology used to help explore and map Earth. It is a computer-based technology that allows people to quickly combine different types of information collected from a specific area. This information helps to create a variety of thematic maps by using information, such as population density, rainfall, elevation, or average temperature. GIS technology can help

scientific investigations, management of natural resources, cartography, and city planning.

As technology improves, so will the maps of our world. The better maps we have, the better equipped we will be to further unravel the mysteries hidden in this dynamic planet.

For helping explorers navigate the planet, uncovering hidden treasures, and providing information to help us work towards a sustainable future, maps are indispensible tools for geology.

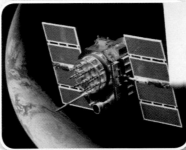

✓ **Check for Understanding**
How is mapping technology evolving to help give us a greater understanding of Earth?

Types of Maps

There are many types of maps, each designed for a specific purpose. Some of the most common are:

Types of Maps Photo Gallery
Learn more about the many ways maps display a variety of information.

Physical Reference Map

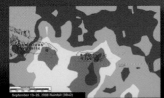

Cantabria, Spain

Shows key physical features of the land, such as rivers, mountains, and deserts. Physical reference maps use color, shading, lines, and symbols to show elevation and landforms.

Political Map

Central Asia

Shows lines defining the borders of countries, states, or territories. A political map shows which areas of Earth belong to a particular country or state.

Thematic Map

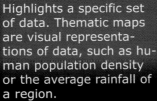

Regional Rainfall Map

Highlights a specific set of data. Thematic maps are visual representations of data, such as human population density or the average rainfall of a region.

Topographic Map

Glenrio

Shows the surface features of Earth. Contour lines represent the topography of the land by linking points on a map that are equal in elevation.

Parts of a Map

Maps are critical tools in the process of exploration and discovery. Cartographers create maps to help people get where they are going, to organize information, or to help make important decisions about how to use resources. When designing maps, cartographers use certain components, called conventions, which should be standard on every map. These conventions allow people to read maps efficiently and effectively.

Title A map's title explains the subject of the map or the information the map contains.

Compass Rose A compass rose is a circular diagram which illustrates the cardinal directions of N, S, E, and W on a map. Intermediate directions of NE, NW, SE, and SW are represented by the smaller points on the compass rose. These points of reference allow you to orient yourself so you can find your bearings, locate positions, and determine direction.

Legend Cartographers use a legend to explain the meaning of symbols and colors on the map.

Scale Cartographers use a scale to indicate the relationship between a certain distance on the map and the actual distance on Earth. The larger the map scale, the smaller the area shown. Cartographers use words (one centimeter = one kilometer) or ratios of units to represent scale. For example, on a map with a scale of 1:100,000, one centimeter on the map would be equal to 100,000 cm, or 1 kilometer, on Earth.

Coordinate System

Explorers and map makers must be able to determine the exact location of a place or point on Earth's surface. A map's coordinate system helps the user know the location of specific objects without any guidance from another person. Cartographers divide Earth into a grid of imaginary lines much like those on a football field. Just as the lines on a football field help players, spectators, and officials locate the placement of a football with accuracy, cartographers use lines, called parallels of latitude and meridians of longitude, to help us find locations on the globe. Using lines of latitude and longitude, we can find the exact locations of objects on Earth.

Lines of Latitude This series of imaginary lines runs parallel to the Equator in an east and west direction. These lines indicate distances north and south of the Equator.

Equator This imaginary line divides Earth into two halves–the Northern and Southern Hemispheres.

Lines of Longitude This series of imaginary lines runs in a north and south direction, and establishes positions east or west of the Prime Meridian.

The Prime Meridian This imaginary line runs straight through Greenwich, England, and is known as the zero point. It divides Earth into the Eastern and Western Hemispheres.

 Mapping Lab Download this activity to further test your mapping skills.

YOUR TURN

Download, copy, or print a map of your local region from an atlas or online resource. Use your knowledge of map conventions to include a scale, compass rose, and coordinate system on the map. Then, determine the potential location of a secret treasure. Use the parts of the map to write a set of clues that someone could use to find the treasure. Exchange your clues and map with another student. Can you find each other's treasure based on the clues and map?

Bios/Wikimedia Commons

Map Projections

Earth is a three-dimensional sphere, but most maps of Earth are drawn on a flat sheet of paper. This can pose some problems to cartographers. Just imagine trying to unpeel an orange and laying the peel out on a flat surface without tearing it!

The representation of a three-dimensional space in two dimensions is called a map projection. When making map projections, the distance, direction, size, and shape of the land or water bodies that are represented on a map can be distorted. For example, on some map projections, Antarctica appears as a giant land mass spanning the entire southern portion of the world. Other maps portray Greenland as large as South America! Antarctic and Greenland are not that big. There are many different types of projections that emphasize different aspects of the land, and cartographers need to take these into account when developing their maps.

Mercator

Mercator maps use straight lines of latitude and longitude, which intersect at right angles. They are one of the most commonly used projections. This projection has the effect of making the regions furthest from the equator appear larger than they are.

Robinson

Robinson maps use concave lines of longitude and a curved shape to reduce some of the distortions of Mercator maps. Unlike Mercator maps, all lines of latitude are the same distance apart.

Equal Area/Sinusoidal

Equal area maps show the true relative size of land masses. You may not be used to maps like this, but they do the best job of representing the size of continents relative to each other. However, the distorted latitude and longitude lines make it hard to use this type of map for navigation.

Maps: Mdf/Wikimedia Commons

The Building Blocks
Earth's Rocks and Minerals

"Rocks and minerals are the foundation of our planet. Only by appreciating the rocks around us will we ever truly understand Earth."

—Dr. Mike Wise
Geologist, The Smithsonian Institution

Dr. Mike Wise

Using electron microprobes, scanning electron microscopes, and x-ray diffraction, Mike Wise studies rocks and minerals he collects in the field to determine how they formed. He hopes to apply this information to locate minerals and rocks that can be used in the technology we rely upon every day.

Meet the Researchers Video
Join Mike as he ventures into the depths of a mine and works in his laboratory. Find out why he searches for rocks and minerals.

Geologist, The Smithsonian Institution ●

Read more about Mike online in the JASON Mission Center.

Peter Haydock/The JASON Project

Your Mission...

Search for and discover invaluable rocks and prized minerals hidden deep under our feet.

To accomplish your mission successfully, you will need to

- Identify rocks and minerals and explain how they are classified by their physical and chemical properties.

- Investigate the formation of rocks and minerals.

- Explore the interrelated nature of rocks and minerals and learn how they explain the changes we see on Earth.

Join the Team

Dr. Mike Wise, from the Smithsonian Institution's National Museum of Natural History, and Argonauts (L to R) Cindy Duguay, Maria Marquez, Emily Judah, and Connor Bebb discover amazonite crystals three meters (10 ft) in length, some 20 meters (66 ft) below the surface in the Morefield Mine in Amelia, Virginia. They even discovered a leopard frog that somehow made its way into the mine.

This mine has been a tremendous resource for studying the way certain minerals form from molten rock. Dr. Wise has spent countless hours deep underground in this mine examining the mineral crystals of tantalite, topaz, amazonite, feldspar, garnet, and quartz.

The World Beneath Our Feet

Tying up the laces on his boots and checking the batteries in his safety pack, Dr. Mike Wise prepares to leave the quiet surface world of Virginia. He has seen magnificent emeralds in North Carolina, neon blue tourmalines in Brazil, and crystals seven meters (23 ft) in length from Canadian mines, so he can only wonder what he might find today. Switching on the lamp on his hard hat, he takes his first step into a deep hole in the ground.

With his light illuminating the ladder rungs and rock wall in front of him, he descends 15 meters (49 ft) below Earth's surface. Turning a dark corner, he glimpses his first find, a bright green three-meter-long amazonite crystal! He examines the crystal with his hand lens and considers the unique geologic processes that formed this pegmatite intrusion. Collecting a small sample with a hammer and chisel, he continues his search in lower levels of the mine. Brilliant soccer ball size white topaz and softball size red garnets stick out of the mine walls, ceiling, and floor. Dr. Wise knows that wherever pegmatites occur, they are full of surprises. Documenting all of his finds, he quickly returns to the lab.

At the Smithsonian Institution's National Museum of Natural History, Dr. Wise prepares the samples he collected for analysis. Using cutting-edge tools, he discovers that this area of Virginia was not always so quiet. Clues hidden in the rocks suggest that volcanoes erupted here at one time. These breakthroughs cause Dr. Wise to ask more questions. What more could these new discoveries tell him about the region's geologic history? After recharging his batteries, he packs up his tools. There is only one way to find out.

 Mission 1 Briefing Video Prepare for your mission by viewing this briefing on your objectives. Learn how scientists, like Mike Wise, use clues to better understand how rocks and minerals form and ways we use these resources in our everyday lives.

Peter Haydock/The JASON Project

Mission Briefing

In This Section:

You Will Learn

What is a mineral?

What are different types of minerals and their properties?

How do minerals form?

How are minerals used?

This is Why

Minerals provide evidence about the geologic formation of an area.

Learning about minerals can help us find new and more efficient ways of using them.

Stage 1: Minerals

What is a Mineral?

Whether we realize it or not, everyone in the world relies on minerals. They are in the food we eat; the homes we live in; and the video game systems, computers, and cellular phones we use every day! So, what are minerals? And, why is Dr. Mike Wise traveling the world researching, studying, and trying to find them?

Minerals are naturally occurring, solid substances. They form directly from geologic sources that were not once living. To date, more than 4,000 minerals have been discovered! And new ones are found every year. **Rocks**, on the other hand, are substances made from a variety of materials, including minerals, fragments of other rocks, plants, and even the remains of animals.

Each mineral can be identified using a single chemical formula. Whether the mineral is made of a single type of **atom** or combination of atoms, called **molecules**, the formula is constant. Some minerals can share the same chemical composition. Graphite and diamond, for example, are both made of carbon (C). Groups of minerals can contain very similar formulas, varying slightly between the minerals. The Feldspars group has variations containing potassium ($KAlSi_3O_8$), sodium ($NaAlSi_3O_8$), and calcium ($CaAl_2Si_2O_8$).

All minerals form **crystals**, which are organized and repeating atoms or molecules joined together. This organized repeating pattern is called a **crystal structure**. You can see and taste mineral crystals every time you put salt on your food. Use a hand lens to take a closer look at a few salt crystals. What do you notice?

What Makes a Mineral?

In order to be considered a mineral, five specific criteria must be met.

Occurs Naturally A mineral cannot be a human-made substance, such as plastic. Crystalline solids produced in a lab, such as diamonds, are formed by different processes than how they form naturally. These human-made crystals are not considered minerals.

Formed Directly from Geologic Sources Minerals are formed directly from geologic sources, such as molten rock or the evaporation of salt water. Minerals do not form directly from biological sources. Pearls created by oysters and coal created from the remains of plants are not considered minerals.

Solid A mineral must have a definite shape and volume. For example, water is not a mineral in its liquid form. However, in a naturally-made and solid form, ice is a mineral.

Definite Chemical Composition Minerals have a specific chemical formula. For example, the chemical formula for quartz is SiO_2. Amethyst, citrine, jasper, and agate are all varieties of quartz; therefore, they all have the same base chemical composition with only slight impurities that affect their color.

Forms a Crystal Structure The shape of the crystal structure is reflected by the repeating pattern of atoms or molecules. Glass might appear to be a mineral, but is not because when it forms, the atoms bond in a random manner rather than a repeating structure.

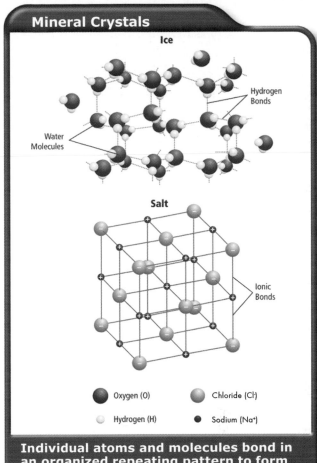

Mineral Crystals

Ice

Hydrogen Bonds

Water Molecules

Salt

Ionic Bonds

- Oxygen (O)
- Hydrogen (H)
- Chloride (Cl⁻)
- Sodium (Na⁺)

Individual atoms and molecules bond in an organized repeating pattern to form the minerals ice (H_2O) and salt, also known as halite (NaCl).

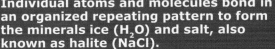

Example

Diamond and graphite are both minerals formed from carbon atoms. However, these minerals have different crystal structures, resulting in very different physical properties. Carbon atoms that form diamonds bond three dimensionally, forming a very rigid crystal structure. Carbon atoms that form graphite bond two dimensionally and are stacked as sheets. This difference in crystal structures is the reason why graphite is soft and often used in pencils, while diamonds are hard and used on the tips of drills.

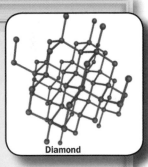

Diamond

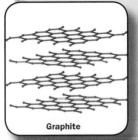

Graphite

Identifying Minerals

When geologists, like Dr. Wise, are in the field or in the lab, they occasionally stumble upon an unknown sample. After examining it with an eye loop or magnifying glass, the geologist will try to identify it. Establishing the identity of a sample requires testing the sample in some key ways.

Each mineral has a distinct set of **physical properties** associated with it. These properties include color, crystal structure, **streak**, **luster**, **density**, **hardness**, **conductivity**, and **cleavage**. Each physical property provides a clue about what mineral it could be. Together, these properties can be used to help identify minerals you see and collect in the field.

Mineralogists have also developed specific methods for classifying minerals. The Dana Classification is the system used most often. It was published in the mid-1800s by James Dana. In 1997, the New Dana Classification system was implemented. The New Dana Classification expanded the original eight classes of minerals to 78 classes.

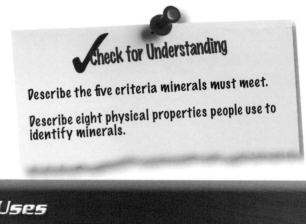

✓ **Check for Understanding**

Describe the five criteria minerals must meet.

Describe eight physical properties people use to identify minerals.

Examples of Minerals and Their Uses

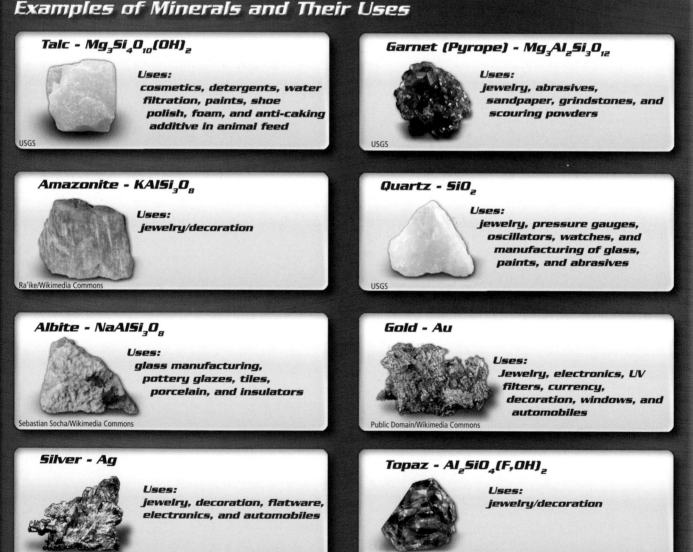

Talc - $Mg_3Si_4O_{10}(OH)_2$

Uses: cosmetics, detergents, water filtration, paints, shoe polish, foam, and anti-caking additive in animal feed

USGS

Garnet (Pyrope) - $Mg_3Al_2Si_3O_{12}$

Uses: jewelry, abrasives, sandpaper, grindstones, and scouring powders

USGS

Amazonite - $KAlSi_3O_8$

Uses: jewelry/decoration

Ra'ike/Wikimedia Commons

Quartz - SiO_2

Uses: jewelry, pressure gauges, oscillators, watches, and manufacturing of glass, paints, and abrasives

USGS

Albite - $NaAlSi_3O_8$

Uses: glass manufacturing, pottery glazes, tiles, porcelain, and insulators

Sebastian Socha/Wikimedia Commons

Gold - Au

Uses: Jewelry, electronics, UV filters, currency, decoration, windows, and automobiles

Public Domain/Wikimedia Commons

Silver - Ag

Uses: jewelry, decoration, flatware, electronics, and automobiles

Public Domain/Wikimedia Commons

Topaz - $Al_2SiO_4(F,OH)_2$

Uses: jewelry/decoration

Archaeodontosauno/Wikimedia Commons

Physical Properties of Minerals

Luster

The way the surface of a mineral reflects light is called luster. Mineral luster can be described as metallic, pearly, vitreous (glassy), greasy (oily), or silky.

Eurico Zimbres/Wikimedia Commons

Color

The chemical composition of a mineral can affect its color. For example, quartz is colorless when pure. However, impurities, like iron, manganese, and titanium, can create a variety of colors, such as blue, yellow, brown, violet, white, red, and pink.

Parent Géry/Wikimedia Commons

Density

Density is the ratio of a mineral's mass to its volume. Iron is denser than graphite because the atoms in iron have a larger mass and are closer together than the atoms that make up graphite.

Streak

Streak is the color of the powder created by rubbing a mineral on a white porcelain streak plate. Some minerals leave a different streak than their general color. For example, hematite can be reddish brown, silver, grey, or black, but it always leaves a reddish-brown streak.

R. Weller/Cochise College

Crystal Structure

The arrangement of atoms or molecules that make up the mineral determines its structure. Examples of mineral shapes include cubes; blocky or brick-shaped; and acicular, which look like a jumble of skinny spikes.

Aelwyn/Wikimedia Commons

Cleavage

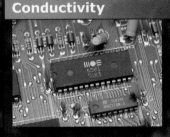

Cleavage refers to how a mineral breaks or fractures along flat planes. A mineral that almost always breaks in a certain direction is considered to have perfect cleavage. A mineral that breaks in a number of planes is considered to have good cleavage.

Walter J. Pilsak/Wikimedia Commons

Hardness

Hardness refers to a mineral's ability to resist scratching. Friedrich Mohs, a German mineralogist, developed the Mohs Hardness Scale to compare minerals to each other. Talc, the softest mineral, is rated 1. Diamond is rated 10, and is the hardest mineral.

Conductivity

Conductivity is a measure of a material's ability to transfer energy, such as thermal or electrical. Minerals containing higher concentrations of metallic elements are generally better conductors of thermal and electrical energy than minerals containing high concentrations of non-metallic elements.

Mineral Formation

Minerals form under specific conditions. If geologists can identify the minerals present in a rock, they can use this information to understand how that rock formed. They can then identify other sources of the mineral by finding locations with similar conditions.

Minerals can form from the cooling of molten rock, from solutions, and from metamorphism. Several factors affect mineral formation, including the chemical composition of the material from which the minerals formed, and the temperature and pressure during formation.

Team Highlight

Argo Emily Judah explores the Morefield Mine in Amelia, Virginia. The mine houses various pegmatite formations, which are of interest to Dr. Mike Wise.

MasterMines Digital Lab Join Argo Emily in a search for valuable minerals around the world and analyze them in your lab.

Minerals from Molten Rock

Dr. Wise studies minerals that form from **molten rock**, a liquid mixture of dissolved pieces of rock, gases, and minerals. Molten rock has two different names, depending upon where it is located. Molten rock located below Earth's surface is called **magma**. If molten rock erupts at the surface, it is called **lava**.

Molten rock can solidify, or harden, when it cools. It hardens as atoms and molecules bond with one another to form mineral crystals. Generally, larger mineral crystals can form when molten rock cools slowly, because atoms and molecules have more time to bond. The terms "larger" and "smaller" are relative, however. Larger crystals can be as big as you are, can fit in your hand, or can be seen without a microscope. Smaller crystals may only be visible with a high-powered microscope.

Magma is located underground and insulated from the cooler air and water at Earth's surface, so it cools and solidifies very slowly. Lava, on the other hand, cools and hardens almost instantly as it comes in contact with water or air, leaving little time for molecules and atoms to bond. Therefore, mineral crystals that formed from magma are typically larger than those formed from lava.

Magma can sometimes produce abnormally large mineral crystals – as large as 11 m (36 ft) long and as heavy as 50,000 kg (55 tons)! Rocks made of these types of mineral crystals are called **pegmatites**. Mike Wise is particularly interested in pegmatites because the minerals they contain are often useful but rare, including beryl, lepidolite, tantalite, and topaz. The large size of these mineral crystals makes them easier and more profitable to mine. By understanding how a pegmatite forms, Dr. Wise can predict other locations where rare minerals may be found.

JEOL JXA-8900R Electron Microprobe

Electron Beam Input Energy: Up to 30,000 Volts

Sample Size: Starts at 1 cubic micron

Data Output: Sample images and chemical composition and concentration

Magnification: 40X to 300,000X

Samples Analyzed at the National Museum of Natural History: Over 10,000 per year

Dr. Mike Wise uses an electron microprobe to analyze mineral samples he collects around the world. This machine can perform multiple tests on each sample.

The scanning electron microscope part of the microprobe first creates an image of the sample for Dr. Wise. He decides which areas should be sampled and selects up to 20 elements the machine should look for. From his analysis, Mike can help determine the commercial viability of a mineral source or predict what other minerals might be found at that location.

The microprobe has been used to study rocks and minerals from around the world, including pegmatite and volcanic rocks. It also has been used to study fossils as old as 505 million years old found in Canadian shale.

Peter Haydock/The JASON Project

The chemical composition of the molten rock can also influence mineral formation. For example, **silicates** are a group of minerals containing silicon dioxide (SiO_2) molecules that form from molten rock. These minerals are the building blocks of most of the rocks we see on Earth's surface. Silicates that form from molten rock rich in silicon dioxide molecules form **felsic** minerals, such as quartz and muscovite mica. If molten rock is low in silicon dioxide content, they form a group of silicates called **mafic** minerals, which include olivine, pyroxene, and amphibole.

Minerals from Solution

When a substance like salt dissolves in water, it is called a **solution**. Solutions are homogenous mixtures of more than one substance, and can be found throughout nature. The air we breathe is a solution. It contains a mixture of substances, such as oxygen, carbon dioxide, and nitrogen. Oceans, lakes, and rivers are also solutions. They contain atoms and molecules from the land around them and the air above them.

Under different conditions, solutions can produce a variety of minerals, such as halite, gypsum, and calcite. Geologists are still studying many of the processes which naturally create minerals from these solutions.

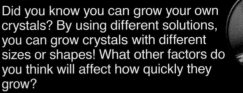

Try This!

Did you know you can grow your own crystals? By using different solutions, you can grow crystals with different sizes or shapes! What other factors do you think will affect how quickly they grow?

Crystal Growing Lab Download instructions on how to grow crystals, and share your findings with your classmates.

Some minerals can form when the liquid in a solution (usually water) **evaporates**. The molecules left behind undergo **crystallization** to make minerals, like halite and gypsum. This is what happened on a very large scale in Bolivia.

The world's largest salt flat, Salar de Uyuni, covers over 9,000 km² (5,600 mi²) in the Potosi region of Boliva. Salar de Uyuni formed as the water from Lake Minchin, a prehistoric salt lake that covered southern Bolivia about 40,000 years ago, dried out. As the water from the lake evaporated, sodium (Na) and chlorine (Cl) atoms combined to form halite (NaCl) crystals. This layer of halite has been measured to be over 10 meters (33 ft) thick at the center of Salar de Uyuni and extends as far as the eye can see!

Minerals can also form by **precipitating** out of a solution. Think back to the salt water. Salt dissolves in water. However, if you keep adding salt to water, at some point the solution becomes saturated and no more salt will dissolve. If you heat the water, you add energy to the system, and therefore, more salt can dissolve. Precipitation of salt crystals occurs when you allow this heated salt water solution to cool. Salt that was once dissolved in the heated water will precipitate out from the solution and collect on the bottom of the container.

This phenomenon occurs at hot springs like the ones in Yellowstone National Park. As the thermally heated water from the underground hot springs reaches the surface and cools, minerals dissolved in the hot water precipitate from the solution.

▲ Large, sword-like gypsum crystals about 275 m (902 ft) below Earth's surface in the Naica Mines of Chihuahua, Mexico were formed over millions of years from solutions heated by magma chambers.

Carsten Peter/National Geographic Image Collection

As calcium-rich solutions flow into caves, impressive looking stalactites and stalagmites can form. A **stalactite** is a mineral deposit shaped like an icicle that hangs downwards from a roof or wall of a cave. **Stalagmites** are mineral deposits that rise upwards from the cave floor. They are usually cone-shaped and form from the dripping stalactites above them.

Stalactites and stalagmites usually form when water, rich in dissolved calcium bicarbonate $(Ca(HCO_3)_2)$, drips from the roof of a cave. When a droplet of this solution is exposed to the air in the cave, it reacts with the air and releases carbon dioxide (CO_2). During this reaction, the droplet deposits a thin film of the mineral calcite $(CaCO_3)$. Over time, these drops will deposit enough calcite to form stalactites and stalagmites.

Minerals from Metamorphism

Minerals can also form through a process called **metamorphism**. These minerals usually form below Earth's surface where temperatures and pressure are very high. Over time, these conditions will metamorphose, or change, the mineral into a new mineral.

Talc, garnet, chlorite, and wollastonite are minerals that can form through metamorphism. Wollastonite can be used in plastics, ceramics, paints, and as a substitute for asbestos. It forms when certain minerals within limestone are raised to high temperatures due to either deep burial or being close to hot molten rock.

✓ **Check for Understanding**
What are five ways minerals can form?

Formation of Minerals

From Molten Rock

Magma

Over time, magma cools, allowing atoms to bond and form crystals. Large mineral crystals can form.
Examples: Quartz, Olivine, Feldspar

Lava

As lava begins to cool, atoms bond and form crystals. Minerals with small crystals can form.
Examples: Pyroxene, Quartz

USGS

From Solution

Precipitation

As solutions become saturated with molecules or chemically react with their surroundings, molecules can crystallize and deposit out of the solution.
Examples: Calcite, Silver

Sam Abell/National Geographic Image Collection

Evaporation

When solutions evaporate, the molecules left behind can crystallize and be deposited as minerals.
Examples: Halite, Gypsum

Ian and Wendy Sewell/Wikimedia Commons

From Metamorphism

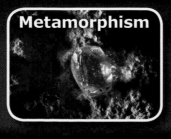
Metamorphism

Minerals beneath Earth's surface under high temperatures and pressures can change into a different type of mineral.
Examples: Jade, Talc, Garnet

Parent Géry/Wikimedia Commons

Mineral Resources

It is amazing how much life on Earth depends on minerals. Single-celled organisms rely on minerals to activate enzymes for growth and survival. Plants absorb minerals from the soil, providing them the food they need to survive. Our early ancestors used minerals, such as chalcedony, to make arrow heads and spears to hunt for animals.

Today, Dr. Wise searches for the minerals which are part of our everyday lives. The roads and highways you took to school today are made from gravel, asphalt cement, and concrete, which contain minerals, such as quartz, feldspar, gypsum, calcite, and mica. Cellular phones and computers require the use of the mineral tantalite in order to work. The insulation used in homes, walls, wiring, and pipes are all made with minerals, like gypsum, feldspar, iron, copper, mica, and quartz.

Metallic Minerals

Some minerals have metallic properties, such as shiny luster, electrical conductivity, and the ability to be molded and stretched. Silver and gold jewelry, copper pennies, and iron used in building supports are all examples of metals.

Many metallic minerals started out as ores. **Ores** are rocks that contain useful minerals that can be mined and sold at a profit. The rocks are mined, and then the minerals are extracted. The value of an ore is dependent on the energy and time it takes to mine and process it, as well as the mineral's value on world markets.

Some ores are formed when fluids, such as water, travel through the cracks and crevices of rocks. When the liquid evaporates, the minerals are left behind in veins. These veins can then be mined.

Gold is an extremely valuable mineral because it is relatively rare and there is a high demand for its physical and chemical properties. Gold does not corrode, crumble, or tarnish, and it is unaffected by moisture, oxygen, and ordinary acids. Because of these qualities, gold is used in technology where reliability is critical. Escape mechanisms in jet planes; devices that detect deadly pollutants, such as carbon monoxide; and air bag systems for cars all use gold wiring.

Fast Fact

What do minerals have to do with video game systems? Minerals are used in a wide range of applications. Tantalum, a rare element found in the mineral tantalite, is used in GPS systems, laptop computers, cellular phones, hearing aids, and the circuitry of some video game systems. In fact, many modern technologies are so dependent on tantalum that shortages can affect how many products can be made. When Sony launched the PlayStation® 2 game console in 2000, the company had difficulty meeting consumer demand due to a shortage of tantalum.

Non-metallic Minerals

Minerals that do not have metallic properties are useful as well. Quartz, a mineral often found in sand, is used to make glass and as part of the timing mechanism of watches. Minerals found in clay are used in porcelain, a material used to make sinks and toilets. The interior walls of some buildings and homes are made with drywall, which is composed mainly of the mineral gypsum.

Explorer's Connection

On an expedition to explore a mysterious deep ocean ridge near the Galápagos Islands, Dr. Bob Ballard and his team of scientists discovered large, tube-like structures called black smokers. These hydrothermal vents spew dark clouds of hot mineral-enriched water, gases, and lava up from beneath Earth's surface. The super-heated water surrounding these vents is saturated with dissolved sulfide minerals. As the water cools, sulfide minerals precipitate out from solution to form the black smokers.

To Dr. Ballard's surprise, these black smokers were surrounded by a large array of previously undiscovered life forms and a variety of minerals, such as gold and silver. Discoveries like these provide us with biologic and economic incentives to further explore our deep oceans.

Gemstone Minerals

You might think of jewelry when you think of diamonds, rubies, and emeralds. However, they are not considered **gemstones** until high grade minerals are cut, faceted, and polished into the forms we see in jewelry and decorations. Many low grade versions of these minerals have a variety of additional uses. Low grade diamonds can be fastened to cutting and drilling equipment, allowing workers to slice through concrete and steel or drill deep into the earth in search of oil and natural gas. Low grade garnet is used in water filtration systems and as an abrasive in sandpaper.

▲ Diamonds found in nature (L) are not considered gemstones until they are specifically cut and faceted (R).

Sustainability

Today, we depend on minerals more than ever. As our reliance on high-tech tools continues to grow, the demand for the mineral resources that support these technologies will increase. To satisfy this demand, we must increase the supply of these minerals. Understanding how and where these minerals form helps geologists identify areas where these resources may exist.

Because most minerals cannot be manufactured, mining is one way we can provide for this demand. However, we cannot depend on mining alone because it can be destructive to natural ecosystems.

Therefore, we must explore other avenues, such as reducing, reusing, and recycling, as we move towards a more sustainable future. Luckily, many minerals can be reused or recycled, including metals in aluminum cans and gold jewelry and the minerals used in cellular phones.

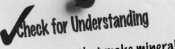

✔ Check for Understanding

Explain the properties that make minerals useful.

Fast Fact

Quartz helps watches keep time. Its crystal structure vibrates when an electric field is applied. The frequency of this vibration is determined by the cut and shape of the crystal. Mechanisms in the watch use these vibrations to time the length of each second. This can then be displayed as either the hands on a clock or the numbers on a digital screen.

Minerals Used in Your Home

Many minerals are used in homes and buildings throughout the world.

- Bricks are made from minerals, such as illite.
- Concrete for the foundation is made from minerals, such as calcite and gypsum.
- Drywall on the inside walls and plaster on the outside is also commonly made from crushed gypsum.
- Nails, bolts, and screws which hold the building together are commonly made from minerals rich in iron, such as goethite and magnetite.
- Plumbing pipes and electrical wires are commonly made from minerals rich in copper, such as bornite and chalcopyrite.
- Glass for the windows is made from the mineral quartz.

Minerals Used in Your Home Explore the minerals that can be found around the house.

Identifying Minerals

When Mike Wise is in a mine or in the lab, he can encounter unknown minerals. To help identify these minerals, he analyzes their properties. Once the minerals have been identified, he can research and develop ideas about the conditions in which each formed. This information helps him understand where these minerals form and potential uses for each.

In this activity, you will analyze the properties of minerals and use a dichotomous key to help determine the identities of several mineral samples. Then, you will conduct research about the geologic conditions in which these minerals may have formed. This knowledge will help you research some current uses of each mineral, as well as possible uses.

Materials
- Lab 1 Data Sheet
- mineral samples
- streak plate
- penny
- magnet
- vinegar
- balance
- water
- graduated cylinder
- hand lens
- nail
- mineral references
- object provided by instructor
- pipette

Lab Prep

1. Your instructor will provide you with an object. Write a detailed physical description of it. Develop a name or category for each part of the description, such as "Color."

2. Trade your object and description with a classmate. Read their description and add anything they have missed. Return the object to your instructor and the description to your classmate.

3. Your instructor will place all of the objects into a box. Using your description, try to identify your object.

4. Document which parts of the description were helpful in identifying the object. Which parts were not as helpful?

5. Modify your description to make it more useful for someone else to use.

6. Return the object to the box and the description to your teacher. Your instructor will provide you with another classmate's description. Use their description to identify their object.

7. Document which parts of the description were helpful and not as helpful in identifying the object. List additional information that would have helped you identify their object.

Make Observations

1. Compare and contrast the categories you made for your object in the Lab Prep to the physical properties of minerals listed in the table on page 17.

2. Obtain a set of minerals from your instructor. As a class, complete steps 3 and 4 on one sample. Then, complete steps 3 and 4 on the remaining samples.

3. Use the Physical Properties of Minerals table and directions in the data sheet to write physical descriptions of the mineral samples.

4. Use your description, the Mineral Dichotomous Key in the data sheet, and the mineral references to identify each sample.

5. Using the mineral references, determine the environment in which each mineral normally forms (from molten rock, solution, or metamorphism).

6. Research and document some uses of the minerals you identified.

7. Describe ways the physical properties of minerals can be helpful to identify minerals in the field and in the lab.

Extension
Collect rocks from your local area, such as the school grounds or around your home. Using the Physical Properties of Minerals table, the Dichotomous Key, and mineral reference books, try to identify some of the minerals in the rocks.

 Journal Question Identify several ways mineral identification can be helpful for scientists, businesses, or agriculture in your local community.

In This Section:

You Will Learn

What is a rock?

What are the different types of rocks and their properties?

How do rocks form and how are rocks used?

This is Why

Understanding and identifying different rocks can provide evidence about the geologic formation of an area.

Stage 2: Rocks

What is a Rock?

What do mountains, valleys, beaches, books, and newspapers have in common? They all tell a story. Books and newspapers are likely places for a story, but have you ever considered the stories of mountains, valleys, and beaches? Understanding these stories is not as straightforward as reading the words in a book. Geologic stories can be told by piecing together the clues found in rocks.

While minerals have a distinct chemical composition, rocks do not. In fact, **rocks** are solids that can be made of minerals, fragments of other rocks, compressed plant matter, and even the remains of animals. The events responsible for changing a rock from its past to current formation can provide insight into the history of Earth. How a rock is formed also determines its classification. Rocks can be classified as igneous, metamorphic, or sedimentary.

Igneous Rock

The word igneous comes from the Latin word *ignis*, which means "fire." **Igneous rocks** are formed from hot molten rock, deep in the earth or erupting at the surface. As this molten material cools, it begins to crystallize into a variety of igneous rocks. The pegmatites Mike Wise studies are a type of igneous rock.

The type of igneous rock that forms from molten rock is influenced by several variables, such as the composition of the molten rock, the pressure, and the cooling rate. Geologists study these different variables in order to learn more about how igneous rocks form.

From Magma

Remember that magma is molten rock beneath Earth's surface. Because temperatures beneath the surface are considerably hotter than at the surface, magma cools very slowly. When magma does eventually cool and solidify, it forms a type of igneous rock called **intrusive rock**. The mineral crystals that make up intrusive rocks are usually large and may be visible without using a hand lens. This is because the slower cooling rate allows them more time to grow and develop.

From Lava

Igneous rocks that form from lava are called **extrusive rocks**. Lava erupts at Earth's surface through volcanoes and oozing fissures. When lava comes into contact with the significantly cooler surface air or water, it cools and solidifies very quickly. Rapid cooling of lava generally results in extrusive rocks with very small mineral crystals, which may only be visible with a microscope.

Some extrusive rocks, like basalt, have cooled so fast that only microscopic crystals are able to form. Volcanic rocks can often have a bubbly texture because gas bubbles in the lava are trapped during the rapid cooling and solidification process.

✓Check for Understanding

Describe the difference between minerals and rocks.

Compare intrusive and extrusive igneous rocks.

Fast Fact

The nose and left cheek of Abraham Lincoln in the Mount Rushmore monument contain a granite pegmatite similar to those Dr. Wise studies.

Scott Catron/Wikimedia Commons

Steve Shattuck/Wikimedia Commons

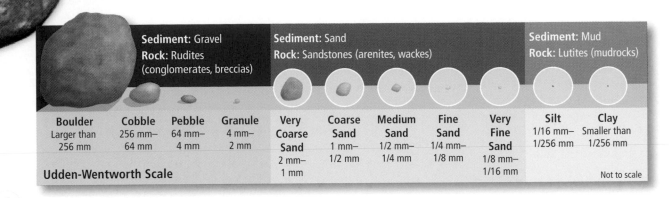

				Sediment: Gravel Rock: Rudites (conglomerates, breccias)				Sediment: Sand Rock: Sandstones (arenites, wackes)					Sediment: Mud Rock: Lutites (mudrocks)	
Boulder Larger than 256 mm	Cobble 256 mm–64 mm	Pebble 64 mm–4 mm	Granule 4 mm–2 mm		Very Coarse Sand 2 mm–1 mm	Coarse Sand 1 mm–1/2 mm	Medium Sand 1/2 mm–1/4 mm	Fine Sand 1/4 mm–1/8 mm	Very Fine Sand 1/8 mm–1/16 mm		Silt 1/16 mm–1/256 mm	Clay Smaller than 1/256 mm	
Udden-Wentworth Scale													Not to scale

Sedimentary Rock

Sedimentary comes from the Latin word *sedimentum*, meaning "to settle." **Sedimentary rock** forms at or near Earth's surface by the settling and accumulation of rocks, minerals, or the remains of plants and animals. **Sediment** can range in size from microscopic clay to large boulders.

Sedimentary rocks are divided into three categories based on the source of the sediment. These categories are: clastic, biologic, and chemical.

Clastic sedimentary rocks form from the accumulation of rock fragments and minerals. **Biologic sedimentary rocks** form from plant or animal remains. **Chemical sedimentary rocks** generally form when minerals precipitate out of a water solution. Precipitation occurs when dissolved minerals recrystallize and separate from that solution.

Formation by Lithification

Picture millions of snowflakes falling from the sky. The first snowflakes to land form the bottom layer of snow. As time passes, layer upon layer of snowflakes gradually accumulate. The weight caused by the built up layers of snow helps to compact them into a snowpack. This snowpack formation is similar to how clastic and biologic sedimentary rocks form. However, sediment is layered instead of snowflakes.

As sediment accumulates over time, sometimes to a thickness of several kilometers, it becomes very heavy and exerts increasing pressure upon the lower layers. Over time this process can squeeze the pieces of rock tightly together. This is the process of **compaction**. You can see evidence of compaction in different layers of colors in sedimentary rock formation.

During compaction, mineral-rich water can seep down around the sediment granules and soak into the sediment layers. Mineral crystals can form around the grains, fusing the sediment pieces together. This process is called **cementation**. Over time, compaction and cementation will form solid sedimentary rock. This entire process of converting loose sediment into rock is called **lithification**.

Example

The Grand Canyon formed from the lithification of sediment and millions of years of crustal uplifting. Over time, layers of sedimentary rock slowly wear away as the Colorado River snakes its way through the canyon, deepening it by about an inch every 500 years.

Sedimentary rock formed by lithification is classified by the material from which it was formed. Clastic sedimentary rocks include shale, which is formed from clay sediment; siltstone, which is formed from silt; and sandstone, which is formed from sand. Sedimentary rocks formed from a combination of rounded pebbles, cobbles, and boulders are called conglomerate. Biologic sedimentary rocks include coal, which is formed from accumulated plant remains, and coquina and chert, which form from the accumulated remains of aquatic animals.

Formation by Dissolving and Re-crystallization

Chemical sedimentary rock is made of mineral crystals that formed from chemicals dissolved in water. The dissolved minerals re-crystallize and form sedimentary rocks through evaporation or precipitation. An example of this is travertine, which forms from geothermal springs and in caves, and is often used as floor tile.

Understanding Change

Investigating rocks can contribute to our understanding of an area's history and the changes it has been through. Sedimentary rocks are generally easy to identify because of their layered structure. Lower layers are usually older and were deposited first. The physical appearance of the layers can reveal the environment in which they formed. Ripple marks indicate that water, such as a lake or an ocean, once covered the sediment. The presence of cracks is evidence that water was present and dried over time, as mud, when saturated with water, tends to crack as it dries.

Sedimentary rock can preserve plant and animal remains. Remains in sedimentary layers provide us with information about the types of organisms present during the formation of the sedimentary rock.

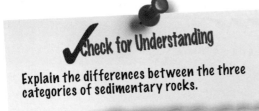

✓ Check for Understanding

Explain the differences between the three categories of sedimentary rocks.

Metamorphic Rock

A rock can go through many changes over time. It can be squished, smeared, and folded by enormous land masses. It can be heated and baked by molten rock rich in dissolved minerals. It can also be subjected to a combination of these processes at the same time! **Metamorphic rocks** are igneous, sedimentary, or pre-existing metamorphic rocks that have changed form. The word metamorphic originates from the Greek *meta*, meaning "change in," and *morphe*, meaning "form." The heat and pressure from deep within Earth is so great that it changes not only the appearance of the rocks, but also the texture and chemical composition of the rocks.

There are two general categories of metamorphic rocks based on their appearances. These are foliated and non-foliated metamorphic rocks.

The banding pattern within this sedimentary rock is caused by environment and composition. How can this information shed light on the changes that have occurred in an area? ▶

James P. Blair/National Geographic Image Collection

Example

Slate, a foliated metamorphic rock, forms when shale, a fine-grained, clay-rich sedimentary rock, is subjected to intense pressure. The pressure causes the tiny grains of clay in the shale to reorient at right angles to the direction of the pressure. The pressure also gives slate a sheet-like appearance.

Foliated Metamorphic Rocks

Foliated metamorphic rocks often have a banded layered appearance. They can form when layers of existing rock, such as shale, get buried under sediment. As more sediment is deposited on top of this layer, the pressure from the weight of the overlying sediment increases. The pressure can increase to a point where minerals within the existing rock are squeezed flat! These flattened minerals change structure and can align to the direction of the pressure. This forms the foliation, or the banded layered appearance that is visible in foliated metamorphic rocks like slate, gneiss, and schist.

Non-foliated Metamorphic Rocks

Non-foliated metamorphic rocks do not have a sheet-like appearance because the minerals that make up the pre-existing rocks do not align under pressure. Non-foliated rocks can form in several ways.

The minerals contained in limestone, a sedimentary rock, do not flatten or stretch regardless of the amount of pressure applied. When limestone is subjected to a combination of both heat and pressure, it forms marble, a metamorphic rock. The heat and pressure smooth out cracks or crevices that may have existed in the original limestone. Marble rocks are highly valued as building and sculpture material because of their smooth texture and color.

Non-foliated rocks can also form through **contact metamorphism**. This occurs when hot molten rock flows into pre-existing rock. The heat introduced by the molten rock bakes the original rock, altering the minerals within it.

Skarn is a metamorphic rock that forms through contact metamorphism of carbonate-rich sedimentary rocks, like limestone or dolostone. When these rocks come into contact with molten rock, the heat transforms them into skarn.

✔ **Check for Understanding**

Compare foliated and non-foliated metamorphic rocks.

▼ **The smooth and beautiful finish of certain grades of marble make it an ideal building material for constructing monuments such as the Anitkabir in Ankara, Turkey.**

Skarn is a metamorphic rock that can sometimes indicate the location of minerals containing valuable elements, such as uranium. Uranium, a radioactive element used to generate electricity, was mined in this skarn deposit located in Queensland, Australia.

Examples of Rocks and Their Uses

Obsidian

Type:
Igneous

Characteristics:
Glassy texture, dark color, microscopic crystals

Uses:
Jewelry, ancient cutting tools

Marble

Type:
Metamorphic

Characteristics:
Smooth texture and color, vitreous luster, low hardness

Uses:
Sculptures, buildings

Basalt

Type:
Igneous

Characteristics:
Fine grains, pale (green, brown, gray)

Uses:
Asphalt roads, ornamental stone statues, floor tiles, roads

Granite

Type:
Igneous

Characteristics:
Medium to coarse grains, crystals highly resistant to breaking

Uses:
Roads, buildings, countertops

Limestone

Type:
Sedimentary

Characteristics:
Fine to coarse grains, even grain size

Uses:
Building material, soil conditioner, insecticides, linoleum, fiberglass

Sandstone

Type:
Sedimentary

Characteristics:
Sand-sized grains, porous, often white, yellow, or brown

Uses:
Building material

Slate

Type:
Metamorphic

Characteristics:
High density, fine grains, foliated texture

Uses:
Building material, roofing

Pegmatite

Type:
Igneous

Characteristics:
Very coarse grains

Uses:
Source of gem minerals and rare elements used in pharmaceutical products, circuits, and electronics

Classifying Rocks Digital Lab
Learn more about and classify rocks from around the world.

Analyzing Rocks and Their Uses _____

In nature, many rocks are made up of a combination of minerals. When Mike Wise is looking for a particular mineral of interest that has commercial value, such as emeralds or tantalite, he looks for certain rocks that are often known to contain the mineral. To help identify rocks in the field and lab, Dr. Wise categorizes them as igneous, sedimentary, or metamorphic. Then he uses a set of descriptions and properties for each category to help further identify the rocks.

In this activity, you will learn about the properties of rocks and apply your understanding to analyze and identify lab grade samples. Then you will use this information to develop a dichotomous key that can be used in the field and lab. Using your key, you will analyze rock samples that are used commercially, such as in buildings or landscaping materials, in your region. This information will help you understand the variety of ways we use rocks in our everyday lives.

Materials
- **Lab 2 Data Sheet**
- **rock samples provided by instructor**
- **digital camera**
- **rock reference materials**
- **computer with Internet access and Google Earth™ installed**

Lab Prep

1 Your instructor will provide you with a set of igneous, sedimentary, and metamorphic rocks and a list of possible names.

2 Write a physical description of each sample using the physical properties of each rock type outlined in the data sheet.

3 Create a dichotomous key of the rock samples according to the directions in the data sheet.

4 Use the list of possible names and rock reference materials to identify each sample. Document the names on the key.

5 Why is it important to use more than one physical property when identifying rocks?

6 Research some commercial uses of each rock sample you identified.

7 Based on your research, predict what types of rocks (igneous, sedimentary, or metamorphic) you might expect to see being used for buildings, landscaping, or other applications around your community.

Make Observations

1 Select a local area where you would like to research the commercial uses of rocks. Obtain a map of the area you are going to research using an atlas, online resources, or Google Earth™.

2 Explore your area to identify human-made objects (such as building and landscape materials) that are made of rocks.

3 Use your dichotomous key and rock resources to try and identify which type of rock is being used (igneous, sedimentary, or metamorphic). If you have enough information, try to identify the rock.

4 Document your observations on your data sheet and on your map. Use a digital camera to photograph each location.

5 Share your results with your class.

6 Download a bedrock map of your state or country.

7 Determine some potential areas in your state or country where the rocks used to make these materials may have come from.

Extension

Create a database of your class's observations by adding placemarks in Google Earth™. For each location, include data about the material analyzed, rock type, photos, and other general notes. Save these placemarks and share them with your class, school, or community to educate them about how rocks are used all around us.

Journal Question Using one of the samples from this lab, write a hypothetical story of how this rock has changed, naturally or through human induced actions, over the last billion years.

In This Section:

You Will Learn
How do rocks change through a process called the rock cycle?

This is Why
The rock cycle shows the relationship between all rock types on the planet.

Stage 3: The Rock Cycle
The Never Ending Story

No matter how a rock is classified today, most likely it won't stay that way. What is now igneous rock could easily become a metamorphic rock. This is because all rocks on Earth go through changes depending on the geologic forces acting upon them. These changes are called the **rock cycle**.

The phrase "rock cycle," however, is a little misleading. Unlike some cycles, such as the life cycle, it is not circular, and rocks can take many different paths. The rock cycle describes all of the processes and forces that transform rocks from one kind to another, and possibly back again! These processes can occur both above and below Earth's surface.

Above Ground

On the surface of Earth, forces like wind, water, and changing temperatures wear down rocks. Given enough time, these forces can break down rocks completely. Over time, rocks which are well below the surface of Earth, such as igneous rocks, can be exposed at the surface. Molten rock can also reach Earth's surface through volcanoes or fissures. Once it does, it will cool, harden, and form into igneous rock. These rocks are then sub-jected to the weathering forces on the surface and can slowly break down into sediment, forming sedimentary rocks like sandstone.

Below Ground

Buried under the massive weight of earth and rock, the environment below Earth's surface can reach extremely high temperatures and pressures. Rocks can change within these harsh environments. With high enough temperatures, rocks can melt and become molten rock. Eventually, molten rock will cool and solidify to become one of a number of types of igneous rocks.

However, not all rocks beneath Earth's surface will melt. Some rocks can change in other ways. Under extreme pressure, the minerals within these rocks can change form. This can result in the formation of metamorphic rocks, such as slate or marble.

 The Rock Cycle Digital Lab Explore the rock cycle further using this online interactive.

Weathering and Erosion of Rocks

Weathering and Erosion of Rocks

Weathering and Erosion of Rocks

Transportation of Sediment

Deposition and Soil Buildup

Burial and Compaction

Sedimentary Rock

Heat and Pressure

Cementation

Metamorphic Rock

Constantly Changing

It is important to understand that with the rock cycle, there isn't a beginning, middle, or end. Rather, the rock cycle is a constant process that continuously builds, transforms, and breaks down rock. Some changes happen faster than others, but the cycle does not stop.

Understanding the processes that can change or affect a rock allows us to develop theories about what might have happened to an area in the past and to predict what may happen to the area in the future. This helps geologists and Argonauts, like you, gain insight into the history of the land beneath your feet.

One Rock's Story

Perhaps the best way to understand the rock cycle is to follow a rock's possible path through it. Granite is an igneous rock formed from cooling magma deep below Earth's surface. Over time, geologic processes may expose it to the surface. Changing temperature, wind, and rain will gradually break the granite into tiny pieces. Tiny pieces of the granite, such as micas, feldspars, quartz, and hornblendes, can turn into fine-grained clays that are carried away by rivers and streams.

Some quartz grains from that granite, however, might break off into larger pieces and become individual grains of sand. Rivers can transport granite sediment great distances across the land, where they slowly accumulate in depressions on Earth's surface called basins. These particles can also wash down rivers to the oceans where they form the deltas and beaches we see at the ocean's edge. This process can take several thousand years.

As more time passes, layers of sediment can slowly build in the basins. These layers of sand-sized sediment undergo compaction and cementation, forming sandstone. As more sediment accumulates, the sandstone might be eventually buried to a depth where heat and pressure from deep within Earth can transform, or metamorphose, the sandstone into quartzite.

The changes do not stop at quartzite. Heat from deep within Earth could melt the newly formed quartzite turning it back into molten rock. It could then solidify again thousands of years later as granite.

Earth is a dynamic planet. While the geologic processes on and in Earth are continuously in action, the rocks and minerals are moving and changing as well. The rock cycle describes the many different paths rocks can take depending on the physical environment that surrounds them and the geologic forces at play.

✓ check for Understanding

What are some of the ways granite can be changed by the forces on and in Earth?

Explain why the rock cycle is never ending.

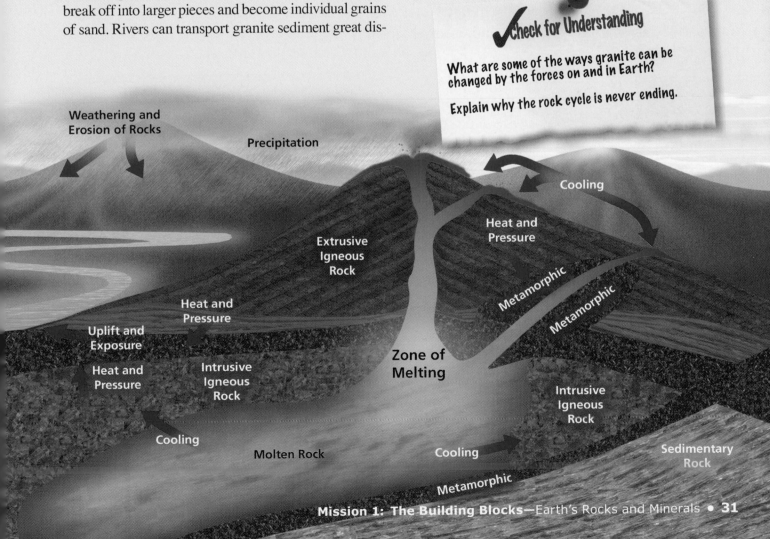

Weathering and Erosion of Rocks

Precipitation

Cooling

Heat and Pressure

Extrusive Igneous Rock

Metamorphic

Metamorphic

Heat and Pressure

Uplift and Exposure

Heat and Pressure

Intrusive Igneous Rock

Zone of Melting

Intrusive Igneous Rock

Cooling

Molten Rock

Cooling

Sedimentary Rock

Metamorphic

Locating Rocks and Minerals

Peter Haydock/The JASON Project

Recall that your mission is to *search for and discover invaluable rocks and prized minerals hidden deep under our feet*. Now that you are fully briefed, it is time to interpret data to identify areas where specific mineral-containing rocks may have formed.

Mike Wise is interested in pegmatites rich in minerals with commercial value. But not all pegmatites contain high levels of these minerals. So, Dr. Wise is trying to better understand the geologic environments which produce pegmatites with high levels of these specific minerals. By understanding these processes, Mike can identify areas of the world where it would be economically practical to mine these rocks.

Once Dr. Wise identifies an area containing pegmatites with large, accessible, highly concentrated minerals, he studies the geologic changes that may have caused them to form in the first place. This research is continuing to uncover the geologic changes that may indicate the presence of pegmatites rich in commercially valuable minerals in other areas of the world.

To begin this assignment, you will analyze Dr. Wise's geochemical data collected from rocks around Sebago Lake in Maine to determine the concentration levels of the element tantalum in different areas. From this analysis, you will determine areas which contain high enough concentrations of tantalum for practical mining. Once you have completed the analysis of Sebago Lake, you will analyze your local geology. Using maps and samples collected in the field, you will develop a model of locations in your area which are economically practical for collecting commercially valuable rocks.

Materials
- Mission 1 Field Assignment Data Sheet
- hand lens
- rock and mineral reference materials
- computer with Internet access

Caution! You must have the landowner's permission to access any land in your study. Even if your study site is on public land, inform the proper authorities of your intent. Obtain permission before collecting samples at your study sites. Never travel alone. Take a responsible adult with you to your study site.

Objectives:

- Analyze the locations of major pegmatite fields in the United States and Canada.
- Analyze maps to determine the topography and types of rocks found at and around the pegmatite fields.
- Analyze geochemical data from pegmatites from locations around Sebago Lake.
- Determine which locations contain pegmatites that are best suited for mining in this area.
- Analyze geologic maps of your local region to determine rock types that are commonly found.
- Observe and collect samples of these rock types.
- Determine areas in your community which contain high concentrations of these rocks, making them economically practical locations for collecting.

Field Prep

1. Analyze the map of major pegmatite fields in the United States and Canada in your data sheet. Identify states, provinces, or areas of the countries that have higher amounts of pegmatites. Determine if there are any pegmatite fields in your local region.

2. Analyze the topographic and bedrock maps of these two countries in the data sheet. Describe the topography and rock types in and around the pegmatite fields you identified in Step 1. Explain any relationships you see between the location of pegmatite fields, bedrock type, and topography.

3. Locate the Sebago Lake pegmatite field on the state map of Maine in the data sheet. This is an area where Dr. Wise has conducted some of his research. Using Dr. Wise's data, you are going to make recommendations for where to efficiently mine for the element tantalum in the Sebago Lake region of Maine.

4. Research the commercial uses of tantalum found in certain pegmatites.

5. Use the bedrock map of Maine in the data sheet to determine which types of rock are at Sebago Lake.

6. Using Dr. Wise's geochemical data from rocks throughout Sebago Lake in the data sheet, make a graph to evaluate potential tantalum mineralization throughout this region.
   - Scatter plot the potassium (K)/rubidium (Rb) ratio on the y-axis and cesium (Cs) on the x-axis using the data. Label each data point on the graph with the location ID.

7. Generally, high levels of tantalum are found in pegmatites with higher levels of Cs and lower K/Rb values. Based on these relationships, make recommendations for which locations should be mined for tantalum by ranking the locations from best (1) to poor (10).

8. Provide an explanation for your ranking of each location. Compare and contrast your rankings with your classmates' rankings.

9. Once pegmatites are located, Dr. Wise must determine how accessible they are for mining. If they are difficult to mine, it may not be an economically practical location. Describe how you would identify new areas to search for pegmatites and tantalum.

Mission Challenge

Using the processes Dr. Wise uses to search for pegmatites, you are going to search for commercially useful and accessible rocks and minerals in your area.

1. Obtain a local bedrock map. Analyze the rock types within a 50 km radius of your school or home. Which types of rock are most commonly found in your region?

2. Pick a local area to explore and obtain a map of this region. Go into the field and collect a variety of different types of rocks and/or minerals, focusing on the type of rocks indicated on the bedrock map. Plot your collection sites and samples on the map. Use your resources to identify the samples you collect.

   a. What type of rocks and minerals did you identify? Note the location of each on your map.

   b. How accessible were the samples during collection?

   c. What are the commercial uses of the rocks and minerals you collected?

Mission Debrief

1. Share your data and map with your class. Using the class data, select the areas in the community which you think may contain the highest concentrations of commercially useful, accessible rocks and/or minerals.

2. Write a proposal to your community leaders about how to best use these resources to the advantage of the community.

 Journal Question Describe how maps and rocks collected from your area can provide you with information about the geology of your local community.

The Chemistry of Diamonds

USGS

Covalent Bond

Weak Binding Forces

Carbon Atom

Graphite

Allotropes of Carbon

Carbon Atom

Covalent Bonds

Diamond

Grab a pencil and write your name on a piece of paper. Take a look at the soft, gray residue on the page. That residue is made out of graphite. Graphite is a mineral, and if the atoms in this graphite were arranged in a slightly different way, the mineral would be a diamond instead. Think about it: you have probably loaned or borrowed pencils several times in your life, but you probably have not done that with diamonds!

Diamond and graphite are what we call allotropes of carbon. Allotropes are substances that are comprised of the same atoms, but the geometric arrangements of the atoms are different, yielding substances with different properties. This is one of the most amazing things about chemistry: something that seems so minor, like the arrangement of atoms, can make a huge difference. Graphite and diamond are only two of several allotropes of carbon.

It is likely that most of the diamonds you have seen are clear and colorless. Diamonds actually come in a variety of colors. In fact, one of the most famous diamonds in the world, the Hope Diamond, is blue. The beautiful blue color that gives the Hope Diamond its value and fame is actually caused by an impurity in the diamond. Small amounts of the element boron got into the carbon crystal structure. Depending on the substance causing the impurity, diamonds can be brown, yellow, green, black, blue, orange, pink, violet, or even

Swamibu/Wikimedia Commons

Victor R. Boswell, Jr./
National Geographic
Image Collection

James P. Blair/
National Geographic
Image Collection

red. Colorless diamonds are by far the most common, so it is fascinating to think that one of the factors that make a diamond unique and special is its "flaw."

In order to get their razzle-dazzle, diamonds used in jewelry have to be cut and polished very carefully. This process demonstrates the beauty of blending art with science. Diamonds need to be cut in a way that works with their crystal structure. A technique called X-ray diffraction is used to determine how the carbon atoms are oriented in space. It can be said that people who cut gems need to learn to speak the language of the atoms they are working with in order to sculpt the diamond's stunning beauty.

Pure diamonds are made of carbon, which is a fairly common substance in the universe. This means that diamonds are not just found on Earth, but that they might also be found throughout the universe. Scientists are now proposing that unique conditions on planets, such as Uranus and Neptune, suggest that there might be lakes made of liquid diamond, with floating, diamond "icebergs!"

So now you know—diamonds are more than just a "pretty" gem. They are "pretty amazing."

Your Turn

Graphite and diamond are not the only two allotropes of carbon. Can you find at least two more? What are they called? How are the crystal structures different from diamond and graphite? What are they used for? Use the Internet or reference materials to help you research, and write a brief paragraph describing what you've found.

"My greatest hope is that people will continue to study and learn about the fascinating interactions between organisms and the geologic environment that supports them."

—Dr. Virginia Dale
Director, Center for BioEnergy Sustainability
Oak Ridge National Laboratory

Dr. Virginia Dale

For the last 30 years, Virginia Dale and her team have studied Mount St. Helens as part of their soil research. Today, her research on how these soils have changed is helping to develop more sustainable methods to efficiently grow food and fuel.

Meet the Researchers Video
Join Dr. Dale and her team at the slopes of Mount St. Helens and as they visit a research farm in Tennessee to learn more about the ecological responses of soils.

Director, Center for BioEnergy Sustainability, ORNL

Read more about Virginia online in the JASON Mission Center.

Peter Haydock/The JASON Project

Your Mission...

Scour Earth's surface for evidence of weathering and erosion – processes that sculpt and shape our ever-changing planet.

To accomplish your mission successfully, you will need to

- Explore the processes of weathering and erosion.
- Compare weathering and erosion.
- Examine landforms and identify the processes that may have created them.
- Analyze soil types and factors that contribute to soil formation.
- Investigate soil conservation techniques and evaluate their effectiveness.

Join the Team

On a cold, windy, and snowy day, Dr. Virginia Dale from Oak Ridge National Laboratory (ORNL) meets the Argonauts (back row L to R) Jennifer Peglow, Karina Jougla, Jodi Phipps, (front row L to R) Ben Brannan, and Sachi Sanghavi in the Toutle River Valley below Mount St. Helens. They examined the soil that is developing after the 1980 eruption. They found that the soils and the ecosystems they support are developing at different rates around the mountain, but that beaver, elk, trees, and shrubs have all returned in great numbers.

Sudden Impact, Gradual Change

"**V**ancouver! Vancouver! This is it!" were the last words radioed by David Johnston to fellow volcanologists at 8:32 a.m. on Sunday May 18, 1980, as he witnessed Mount St. Helens in Washington state erupting. The volcano had the strength of about 500 World War II era atomic bombs, sending around 400 meters (1,312 ft) of the top of the mountain tumbling down into the Toutle River Valley. Volcanic ash rose up to 25,000 meters (15.5 mi) into the atmosphere and 2.3 cubic kilometers (0.55 mi³) of debris collapsed from the north facing slope of the mountain. Scientists estimate that rocks achieved speeds exceeding 240 kilometers per hour (150 mph) as they moved down the mountain.

At the same time, Dr. Virginia Dale was working on a proposal to study the long-term ecology of the Mount St. Helens region. After the explosion, she and her team immediately went to work surveying the volcanic damage. They were surprised to find that a few animals, like gophers and burrowing insects, survived the initial eruption. These animals were already hard at work mixing the ash into the soil as they dug their way to the surface, creating places for seeds to take root and facilitating the formation of new soil.

Thirty years later, at her lab at Oak Ridge National Laboratory in Tennessee, Dr. Virginia Dale still studies Mount St. Helens. With her education in ecology and math and the help of her team, Dr. Dale applies the lessons that she has learned from her work at Mount St. Helens to her current research on biofuels.

While her work at Mount St. Helens involves looking at changes in an environment over time, her biofuels research involves the study of changes in the environment over space. She seeks to determine how much land should be converted to energy crops to maximize the benefits to our society.

Mission 2 Briefing Video Prepare for your mission by viewing this briefing on your objectives. Learn how scientists, like Virginia Dale, use their understanding of weathering and erosion to monitor and explain changes in soils that are used to grow plants for food and fuel.

Mission Briefing

In This Section:
You Will Learn

What is weathering?

Why does weathering occur?

How is the rate of weathering affected by environmental conditions?

This is Why

Understanding the processes behind the weathering of rocks can help explain changes on Earth's surface.

Stage 1: Weathering

What is Weathering?

Even though we may not notice it, the surface of our planet is in a constant cycle of change. Throughout Earth's existence, geologic processes have been slowly building landforms, while weathering and erosive forces have worked to constantly shape, carve, and wear these landforms away.

Weathering is a process that gradually breaks down materials, such as rocks and minerals. **Erosion** is the process of moving sediment from one place to another, usually by wind, water, gravity, or a combination of these forces. Together, weathering and erosion drive the rock cycle on or near the surface of Earth by breaking down and transporting rocks. Given enough time, weathering and erosion can transform the land by carving valleys, tearing down cliffs, and even flattening mountain ranges!

▲ Wind, water, and gravity have shaped the cliffs of Victoria, Australia over time, resulting in the land formation we know as the Twelve Apostles.

Ryan Kincade/The JASON Project

These forces can also have a great effect on the plants and animals living on Earth. Geologists and ecologists, like Dr. Virginia Dale, study how weathering and erosion impact the chemistry and other qualities of soils that we use to grow food and bioenergy crops. Dr. Dale's research helps to produce ethanol, a fuel used by cars, more efficiently from renewable resources like switchgrass.

Types of Weathering

How do you know a rock is being weathered? Just take a look. It can look like it is starting to crumble. Cracks might be present, or the color might be changing. How exactly is the rock being broken down? There are two categories of weathering, mechanical and chemical.

Mechanical weathering is a process of physically breaking materials, such as rocks, into smaller pieces without altering the chemical composition of its components. **Chemical weathering** is a process that changes materials, such as rocks, by altering the chemical composition of its components. These two processes can work together or alone, at or near Earth's surface to break down rocks.

▲ Even the hardest rock can crack under the constant force of weathering.

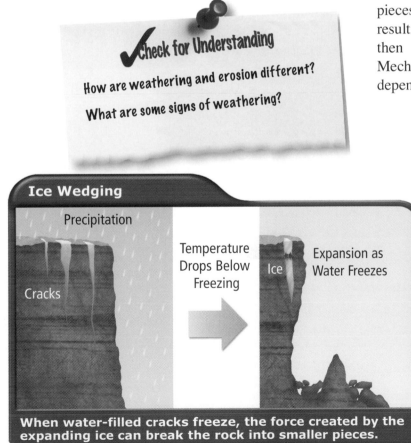

✔ Check for Understanding

How are weathering and erosion different?

What are some signs of weathering?

Ice Wedging

Precipitation

Cracks

Temperature Drops Below Freezing

Ice

Expansion as Water Freezes

When water-filled cracks freeze, the force created by the expanding ice can break the rock into smaller pieces.

Mechanical Weathering

If someone took a sledgehammer to a rock, what do you think would happen? You would probably end up with a big mess! Upon closer examination of this "mess," you might notice that the minerals making up the pieces of rock are the same as its **parent material**, the original material from which the rubble came. This is how mechanical weathering works.

Mechanical weathering breaks rocks into smaller pieces without changing them chemically. If the resulting pieces of rock match their parent material, then mechanical weathering has taken place. Mechanical weathering occurs in a variety of ways depending on the environmental conditions present.

Freezing and Thawing

Water can fill cracks in a rock. When temperatures drop below 0°C (32°F), the water freezes and turns to ice. As water freezes, it expands. The outward force caused by the expanded ice widens the cracks in the rock. When the temperature increases, the water thaws and the cracks can refill with water. Over time, the cycle of water filling cracks, freezing, expanding, thawing, and refilling acts as a wedge by slowly widening the crack until the rock breaks. This process is known as **ice wedging**. Evidence of ice wedging can often be seen on mountains as giant cracks in a slab of rock. Ice wedging is also the main cause of potholes in roads during the winter.

Siim Sepp/Wikimedia Commons

▲ The striations on this rock were caused by glacial abrasion.

Abrasion

Abrasion occurs when rock is gradually scraped and sanded down by particles carried by water, wind, or ice. Sediment carried by flowing water can collide and gradually grind away rocks in a streambed. Sediment can also be carried by wind or slow moving glaciers. Over time, this sediment can carve and shape the land.

Exfoliation

Exfoliation occurs when outer layers of rocks flake off. This is caused by changes in pressure or temperature that lead to the expansion or contraction of rocks.

Exfoliation can occur when a rock expands after a massive weight is removed. For example, glaciers can compress rocks beneath them. As the glacier recedes and is no longer on top of the rock, the compressed rock begins to expand. This sudden expansion can cause some of its outer layers to crack and flake off.

Rocks in environments with large daily temperature changes can also undergo exfoliation. In this case, the mechanical weathering is caused by thermal expansion and contraction. Sunlight can cause rocks to heat to very high temperatures. When rocks are heated, they expand. At night, rocks contract as temperatures drop. This daily cycle of heating and cooling, expansion and contraction, can lead to exfoliation.

Living Organisms

Living organisms can also cause weathering. Tree roots can find their way into the cracks of rocks, widening the cracks as the trees grow. Burrowing animals, like moles, gophers, and some insects, can also gradually loosen and break apart rocks in the soil.

When Mount St. Helens erupted and covered the region with ash and other volcanic debris, much of the ecosystem was devastated. Dr. Dale's research shows that living organisms are playing a critical role in revitalizing the region as they mechanically weather their surroundings. For example, the gophers that survived the volcanic eruption deep in their underground burrows are now helping to mix and churn volcanic ash, soil, and rock. This has distributed the nutrients in the soil evenly, and has helped make the ground suitable for the life that has sprouted in the region over the past 30 years.

✓ Check for Understanding

Identify and describe three examples of mechanical weathering.

How can heating and cooling cause weathering?

As this tree continues to grow and develop, its roots will slowly weather away the rocks used to construct the ancient temple.

David Alan Harvey/National Geographic Image Collection

Chemical Weathering

Weathering also occurs when chemical interactions change the chemical structure or composition of minerals within a rock. These changes can often lead to the breakdown of rocks.

Oxidation

Oxidation is a chemical weathering process commonly known as rusting. It occurs when rocks and minerals are exposed to oxygen. Oxygen (O_2) reacts with certain minerals, changing their chemical composition and structure. This change can be accelerated in environments of high moisture and temperature.

A common example of oxidation involves rocks containing iron (Fe). Iron will begin to oxidize when exposed to oxygen, altering its chemical structure to iron oxide (Fe_2O_3), a reddish brown rust. As iron within a rock is oxidized, the rock is weakened, causing it to crumble easily.

▲ This piece of sandstone is gradually oxidizing from the outside in.

Exposed Stone
flaking off with acid rain damage

Unexposed Stone
not affected by acid rain

Hole
caused by acids in rain reacting with limestone

Hydrolysis

Hydrolysis occurs when minerals react with ions, such as hydrogen (H^+) from water. For example, when rain water comes into contact with silicate minerals, new minerals may form. This reaction can cause large rocks to break into smaller pieces or to change into silts or clays.

Living Organisms

A lichen is often thought of as a plant, but it is actually part fungus and part alga. It can survive in some of Earth's most extreme environments. It has been found growing in the arctic tundra, high mountain tops, and in harsh deserts. It could even survive in space!

When attached to rocks, lichens can secrete a weak acid that dissolves some of the minerals in the rock. These dissolved minerals provide the lichens with some of the nutrients that help them grow.

▲ Weak acid secreted by lichens can chemically weather a rock.

Carbonation

Carbonation occurs when carbon dioxide (CO_2) dissolves in water (H_2O), forming carbonic acid (H_2CO_3). This chemical reaction occurs naturally in the atmosphere as water and atmospheric carbon dioxide mix. When this happens, it produces the weak acid known as **acid rain**.

Chemical weathering results when acid rain falls on and seeps into the cracks of rocks rich in minerals that react readily with acid, like calcite ($CaCO_3$). The acid rain causes a chemical reaction to occur which breaks down the calcite. The effects of acid rain can be seen in many old buildings, statues, and tombstones that were constructed using limestone and marble, which are both rich in calcite.

✔ Check for Understanding

Describe some evidence of chemical weathering.

How is acid rain produced?

Evidence of Weathering

Mechanical Weathering

Abrasion

Siim Sepp/Wikimedia Commons

The constant scraping and sanding by sediment particles carried by wind and water have gradually given this igneous rock face in western Norway a smooth polish.

Exfoliation

Bryan Ie/The JASON Project

An unearthed stone situated on Old Rag Mountain in Virginia is beginning to show the effects of constant heating and cooling.

Living Organisms

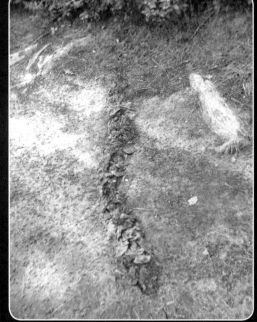

Jomegat/Wikimedia Commons

Burrowing animals, like gophers, can mechanically weather rocks as they dig through the earth. These actions can help mix soil and aid in making it rich and fertile.

Freezing and Thawing

Public Domain/Wikimedia Commons

Steep pyramidal shaped mountain peaks, like the Matterhorn in Switzerland, have resulted from freezing and thawing over time.

Wolfgang Staudt/Wikimedia Commons

Chemical Weathering

Living Organisms

Lichens capture nutrients by secreting weak acids that dissolve minerals in rock. They can also harness the sun's energy, allowing them to live almost anywhere.

George F. Mobley/National Geographic Image Collection

Hydrolysis

These cliffs on Maria Island, Tasmania, have been shaped by a number of processes, including hydrolysis. Hydrolysis occurs when water reacts with rock, slowly turning a cliff into sediment, like clay and sand.

Noodle Snacks/Wikimedia Commons

Carbonation

Carbonation occurs when carbon dioxide dissolves in water. When this happens, the water increases in acidity and can dissolve the calcium carbonate that composes rocks such as limestone. This process often occurs beneath the surface, and sinkholes may result when the ground finally collapses due to the loss of underlying support material. Builders must consider the possibility of sinkholes if they build where limestone rocks are widespread.

Federal Emergency Management Agency

Oxidation

The reddish hue on the surface of these rocks indicates the iron minerals that make up these rocks are undergoing oxidation, a chemical reaction that produces rust.

Nicholas/Wikimedia Commons

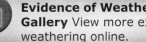

Evidence of Weathering Photo Gallery View more examples of weathering online.

Exploring Weathering

When Virginia Dale and her team of researchers arrived on the slopes of Mount St. Helens after the eruption, they made many preliminary observations. A majority of the vegetation, such as trees, bushes, and grass, was destroyed. While the surface was covered with ash from the eruption, it was more exposed to the many processes of weathering. Over the next 30 years, Virginia and her team observed and monitored these weathering processes to determine their effects on the vegetation and animals which repopulated this mountain ecosystem.

In this activity, you will experiment with a variety of weathering processes in order to understand the different types of weathering and the factors that may affect the rate at which they happen. Then, you will go outside and look for signs of weathering in your local area. Based on your observations, you will develop models for what this area may look like in the future.

Materials
- Lab 1 Data Sheet
- materials provided by instructor
- digital camera or drawing pad

Lab Prep

1. With your instructor, review the objectives and procedures for each weathering experiment.

2. Review all appropriate safety guidelines and classroom rules for each experiment.

3. Use the materials and equipment provided to perform each experiment.

4. After conducting each experiment, determine the type of weathering you observed and what factors may be affecting the rate of weathering.

Make Observations

1. Go outside and look for evidence of mechanical and chemical weathering around you.

2. Document where you are and what you think is occurring. Use pictures, video, or drawings to record your observations.

   a. Describe the material or object being weathered.

   b. Is the weathering occurring on the material or object natural or human-induced?

   c. Is the weathering on the material or object being influenced by natural or human-made objects near or around it?

3. Based on your observations, hypothesize about what some of these areas or objects will look like in 100 years, based on the natural or human-induced effects of weathering.

4. Develop a potential method for monitoring the weathering in these areas or on these objects over time.

5. Present your monitoring method to your class.

Extension

Implement your method for monitoring weathering over time in your local area. Present your findings to your class.

 Journal Question Discuss some factors that may influence how materials weather.

Bruce Dale/National Geographic Image Collection

Rates of Weathering

Earth is a big object made of many different types of rocks and minerals. At any given moment, there is someplace where it is sunny, rainy, windy, humid, dry, hot, or cold. There is a place where someone is walking, a river is running, an animal is digging, plant roots are growing, and water is dripping, freezing, or thawing. Environmental conditions constantly bombard rocks at different intensities, affecting the rates at which they weather.

Most weathering does not happen overnight. It is a gradual process that occurs over hundreds, thousands, and even millions of years.

▲ Weathering and erosion in the Gulf of St. Lawrence, Canada have sculpted Percé Rock, one of the world's great natural arches.

▲ The rate of weathering is affected by different factors, leading to unique desert rock formations.

Type of Rock

Each type of rock has a unique set of **physical properties**. These physical properties affect the way it reacts to certain conditions and ultimately affects the rate at which it weathers.

The type of rock and the environmental conditions to which it is exposed are two of the main factors that affect how fast weathering occurs on a specific rock. In an environment bombarded by the abrasive forces of wind, water, and ice, a harder rock, like granite, will weather more slowly than a softer rock, like sandstone. If acid rain is present, limestone will wear away a lot faster than other rocks due to the calcite in the limestone.

Surface Area

Surface area is the measure of area on the outside of an object, such as a rock. The surface area of a rock can affect the rate at which it weathers. Generally, the greater the surface area of a rock, the faster it will weather. As a rock weathers, it may begin to form cracks. Over time, continual weathering will increase the size of these cracks, which in turn, will increase a rock's surface area as more area is now exposed to the outside. This process can compound over time and can eventually lead to the breakdown of the rock.

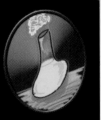

Try This!

Measure the surface area of two sugar cubes. They should both have very similar surface areas. Wrap one of the sugar cubes in plastic wrap and place both in a glass filled with warm water.

Observe and explain the role that exposure has on the rate at which the cubes dissolve.

Exposure

Uncovered rocks are exposed to elements, such as wind, rain, sunlight, freezing, and thawing. These rocks will generally weather much faster than those covered by soil, water, or ice. For example, a large boulder that is mostly buried may not weather as quickly as a smaller rock that is lying on top of the ground.

Math Connection

If a 10 cm (3.9 in.) layer of sandstone weathers at a rate of 1 cm (0.4 in.) every 100 years, how long would it take for it to completely break down?

1 cm / 100 years = 10 cm / x years

Solving for x, it would take 1,000 years!

How long would a blade of grass take to grow 10 cm if it grew at the rate of 1 cm per day?

IFE/COEAO

David Boyer/National Geographic Image Collection

▲ Clearing the land of vegetation for the construction of roads, buildings, and mines can drastically increase weathering rates.

Climate

Climate is the combination of temperature, humidity, rainfall, and sunlight at a given region on Earth. Different combinations of these factors affect the rate at which rocks weather.

Hot and humid conditions accelerate the oxidation process of rocks containing iron. Large fluctuations in daily temperatures can result in the continual expansion and contraction of rocks. These areas will exfoliate rocks faster than areas where temperatures are more constant.

Regions of heavy rainfall will weather sedimentary rock, such as sandstone, much faster than dry climates. Weathering rates also increase in regions of the world that experience acid rain.

Human Activity

Human activities can be the biggest influence on weathering rates. For example, clearing land for the construction of roads and building projects using bull dozers and dynamite may accelerate weathering. What may have taken millions of years to naturally break down, happens in a matter of days or weeks due to human activity.

Landscaping and agricultural practices can unearth rocks that were once protected by layers of soil. Mining breaks down rocks deep within Earth and brings them up to the surface. Clear cutting of forests can also influence the way rocks are exposed to the different elements of nature. Trees that once shielded rocks and minerals from weathering are removed, leaving the rocks and minerals exposed. These activities all work to accelerate the exposure of rocks to natural elements, like wind, rain, sunlight, temperature, and acids. Increased exposure to the elements ultimately leads to increased weathering rates.

Industrialization also affects weathering rates. As our need for energy increases, so does the carbon dioxide released into the atmosphere. This greenhouse gas contributes to the formation of acid rain, which can cause weathering.

Peter Haydock/The JASON Project

✓ Check for Understanding

What factors contribute to the rate of weathering, and how?

This is Why

Understanding and identifying the forces that drive erosion can help explain the diverse landforms on Earth.

Stage 2: Erosion
What is Erosion?

Erosion is the process that moves, transports, and deposits loosened rock particles, or **sediment,** away from the original rock. Erosion usually works together with weathering. As weathering slowly wears down and loosens rock, erosion carries away the loosened particles.

The movement and transport of sediment occurs in many different ways. It can be caused by gravity or in combination with a variety of other factors, such as water and wind. These factors combine to continually shift, move, transport, and deposit rock particles weathered by mechanical and chemical processes.

The effects of erosion can be seen through the movement and **deposition** of sediment. It can be seen in the wind carved sedimentary rock formations in the desert, the rolling rocks lining a river bed, or even the stalactites lining the roof of a cave. All of these features are the results of agents of erosion at work in a particular environment. There are several different agents of erosion.

▲ The constant forces of water and wind slowly erode this towering rock face of the Grand Canyon.

Surface Water

Water is a powerful agent of erosion that can start as a simple drop of rain. A tiny raindrop can loosen small particles such as clay sediment. Raindrops can combine with other drops to form a trickle of water. This trickle can merge into slightly larger streams that loosen and transport more sediment. As streams merge into one another, they form a river.

As a river or stream flows, it will create a path by weathering and eroding away soft layers of rock, like sandstone. Sometimes, rivers will encounter layers of rock that do not weather and erode as easily, such as granite. This can cause rivers to change course, or **meander,** as rushing water tends to flow in the direction of least resistance. However, even harder layers of rock, like granite, can be eroded by flowing water over time.

Surface water can be so powerful that it can even transport giant boulders downstream. Surface water can also spread sediment when rivers overflow their banks. This is called **runoff** and generally occurs because of heavy rainfall.

Sediment particles can travel great distances when moved by surface water. However, if water carrying sediment flows over a depression or basin, its load of sediment can be deposited. If water meets an obstacle or has to spread out over a larger area, it might not have enough energy to carry its full load of sediment

and will deposit it. Over time, sediment particles can gradually accumulate and can eventually form sedimentary rock.

Groundwater

Not all water is found on top of Earth's surface. Some water from rainfall and snowmelt is also absorbed by the earth and is called **groundwater**. Groundwater is the water found beneath Earth's surface that soaks into cracks and crevices in soil and rock. Carbon dioxide trapped in the soil can dissolve into the groundwater. The groundwater then becomes an acidic solution capable of dissolving and carrying away underground limestone deposits formed from the shells and skeletons of ancient marine organisms.

▼ Water rushing over the rocks and riverbed of the Potomac River has created a series of waterfalls on the Maryland-Virginia border known as Great Falls.

In some cases, so much limestone is dissolved and eroded away that a cave begins to form. Given enough time, this process can result in massive underground caverns and rivers. Often, the caverns created are lined with stalactites and stalagmites. This occurs when limestone dissolved in water seeps through cracks in the rock walls and is re-deposited as stalactites and stalagmites.

In some regions of the world, underground valleys and caves are fairly common. The right environment of acidic soil, usually layers of limestone or dolomite **bedrock**, and rainfall can produce a unique type of landform called **karst topography**. As the limestone or dolomite is dissolved by acidic groundwater, layers of earth are hollowed out to form caves.

Karst topography can be dangerous. The dissolved bedrock can be weakened and can suddenly collapse, creating a sinkhole.

Glaciers

Glaciers are large masses of ice, snow, water, and sediment that originate on land. They can be extremely powerful erosive forces. Glaciers move due to the pull of their own weight. As a glacier moves, it erodes the land by picking up sediment ranging from grains of sand to giant boulders. Sediment particles carried by a slow-moving glacier can act like a giant sheet of sandpaper, weathering the land beneath.

Over time, a glacier will eventually melt, leaving behind the evidence of its erosive path. For example, glaciers can erode the land to form U-shaped valleys. When a U-shaped valley fills with sea water, it is called a **fjord**.

Ester Inbar/Wikimedia Commons

▲ Waves and tidal action deposit sediment that has been eroded from elsewhere, building sandbars.

Waves

Waves can contribute to erosion in a variety of ways. For example, the sheer force of waves continually bombarding a shoreline can weather rocks over time, breaking them up into pieces of loose sediment. Erosion occurs when waves carry bits and pieces of sediment away, and deposit them to form sandbars and beaches.

The land formations caused by the erosive effects of waves can be unique. Softer rocks, like sandstone, weather and erode faster than harder rocks like granite and basalt. When there are layers of harder and softer rock, the softer rock will erode quicker, which can form headlands.

Sediment from eroding shorelines is carried away by ocean currents and deposited on beaches. You may have noticed that different beaches have different types of sand. Sand characteristics are determined by the type of rocks from which the sand was formed. White

Landform Detectives Digital Lab Join Bob Ballard, and try to identify what geologic processes have created landforms we see today.

James P. Blair/National Geographic Image Collection

▲ Black sandy beaches result from the weathering, erosion, and sedimentation of basalt.

sand beaches may be composed of quartz particles. Some beaches have an olive green tinge because it is eroded sediment from the parent material olivine. Other beaches may be covered in black sand due to the erosion of black igneous rock called basalt.

Wind

Wind can be a powerful force. Just take a look at a playground on a windy day. The wind can push an empty swing back and forth. Stronger winds can tip trash cans and flower pots, causing garbage, paper, soil, and plant debris to scatter throughout the grounds. Wind can also be an effective agent of erosion and change Earth's surface.

Wind can erode vast expanses of land where surface material, like soil, is not anchored down by plant roots. Deserts are usually susceptible to wind erosion because very few plants are able to live there. Without the stability provided by a plant's root system, movement of soil and sediment is more common.

The process of wind erosion occurs through deflation. **Deflation** is the gradual removal of loose surface material by wind. When loose surface material, like grains of sand, is picked up by the wind, it results in shallow depressions in the ground. Stronger winds can move larger-sized sediment by rolling them great distances.

As sediment is carried away through deflation, additional rocks can be weathered through abrasion, or the scraping of rock caused by particles. Both deflation and abrasion can work simultaneously to slowly polish, carve, and shape rock structures.

When winds slow down or when grains of sand carried by the wind collide with an object, such as a plant or a boulder, the sediment will fall to the ground. Gradually, more sediment will hit this obstacle and begin to accumulate. The accumulation of sand-sized particles can eventually form a sand **dune**.

▼ Swirling winds makes endless shapes and patterns in desert sands, often resulting in huge sand dunes.

✔ Check for Understanding

How does sedimentation and deposition change the surface of Earth?

Desert Formations Over Time

Plateau   Fin   Window   Hoodoos

Desert formations, like fins, windows, and hoodoos, form because they contain a cap of hard, weather resistant rock. Over time, wind and water will weather and erode surrounding softer layers of rock faster, leaving behind these desert sculptures.

Mass Movement

Sometimes, gradual weathering and erosion of the landscape combine with gravity to produce drastic and noticeable changes. These changes can happen in a matter of seconds. You may have seen news reports capturing images or video footage of landslides, rock falls, or mudflows. Other times, large chunks of land slowly move down a slope. Regardless of the time it takes to happen, whenever earth material is transported down a slope by gravity, it is called **mass movement**. Types of mass movements include **landslides**, **rock falls**, **mudflows**, **slumps**, and **creeps**.

✔ **Check for Understanding**

Describe three types of mass movement.

When is mass movement dangerous?

USGS

A **landslide** is the downward movement of rock, soil, mud, or various combinations of material. It can start with the smallest clay-sized particle and eventually lead to great masses of land moving down a slope.

USGS

Rock falls occur when sediment of any size free falls from a cliff. They are common on roads cut into cliffs. To help prevent damage from falling rocks, road engineers may bolt layers of rocks into place, cover them with wire nets, or construct protective screens.

USGS

Mudflows occur when water mixes with rock debris and soil until the land absorbs enough water so that it becomes the consistency of wet cement or mud. If a mixture like this develops on a slope, a mudflow can occur. Mudflows can move with surprising speed.

Jim McDougal/Wikimedia Commons

A **slump** is the down slope movement of an intact mass of rock and soil. Unlike a landslide, the mass of rock does not crumble into little pieces, but remains more or less together and travels as one large mass.

Salem State

Creep is the slow movement of soil and rock down a slope. It can be such a gradual process that it may take years to notice. Trees often provide evidence of creep, as the downward creep of soil and rock can result in strangely curved tree trunks.

Erosion Modeling

When Mount St. Helens erupted in 1980, thousands of kilograms of sediment were quickly eroded during the blast. Some sediment was transported via the Columbia River to the Pacific Ocean. When Virginia Dale and her team arrived on the mountain, they also saw evidence of other types of erosion. As the heat from the eruption melted the snow into water, the water quickly moved down the mountain. This water quickly eroded large areas and deposited sediment, some ten meters (32.8 ft) deep, throughout the area surrounding the mountain.

In this activity, you will construct a model landscape that will be subjected to the forces of erosion and deposition. Using this model, you will investigate and monitor the levels of erosion and deposition within different areas of the landscape.

Materials
- Lab 2 Data Sheet
- stream table
- polystyrene or paper cup
- water container
- craft stick
- sand
- rocks
- stream table supports
- ruler
- string
- masking tape
- clay

Lab Prep

1. Set up the stream table as outlined in the data sheet.

2. Add structures, such as rocks or levees, to the sediment (sand) and document the location of these on your data sheet. Draw the landscape on your data sheet.

3. Set up a labeled grid on the top of the stream table as outlined in the data sheet.

4. Starting with 0 at one end, use a pen to mark 0.5 cm increments on your craft stick.

5. With 0 at the bottom, push the craft stick straight down into the sand at each grid location. Document the initial height of the sand at each location on your data sheet.

6. Smooth the surface of the sand at each grid location where the craft stick was placed.

7. Determine and document on your data sheet the location where the water will pour into the stream table. Before pouring the water, predict which areas will have high or low levels of erosion, and which areas will have high or low levels of deposition.

Make Observations

1. Position the cup and run the model by filling the cup with water from the water container. Make sure you continue to refill the cup as it empties. Document your observations as the model runs.

2. When the model is done running, determine the height of the sand at each grid location using your stick.

3. Identify areas of high and low erosion and deposition.

4. Document the amount of erosion and deposition that took place at these locations by determining the change in elevation between the initial and final heights.

5. Compare and contrast your predictions in Lab Prep step 7 with the results.

6. Identify some of the variables that may be influencing erosion and deposition in the areas you identified.

Extension
Repeat the experiment changing one of the following variables: shape of your initial landform, composition of your sediment, placement of starting water flow, or placement of added structures. Share your results with your class.

Journal Question Why should communities be aware of areas of erosion and deposition in their local area? Recommend some strategies for monitoring erosion and deposition in your area.

Earth's Varied Geology

Receding glaciers can scrape, carve, and shape the land, leaving behind **pyramidal mountain peaks**, U-shaped **valleys**, **moraines**, and **drumlins**. Ice-wedging, water, wind, and gravity can further weather rocks, forming steep mountain faces and causing mass movement.

Flowing rivers fed by rain and melting ice help to carve V-shaped valleys. Rivers also carry sediment from the weathering and erosion of rocks. This sediment can be deposited to form **deltas** and **sandbars** located at **river mouths**.

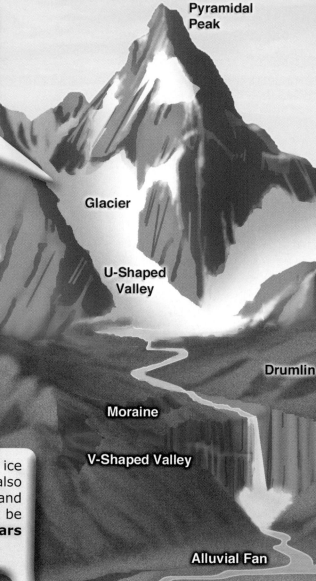

Pyramidal Peak

Glacier

U-Shaped Valley

Drumlin

Moraine

V-Shaped Valley

Alluvial Fan

Beach

Delta

River Mouth

Sandbar

Nothing on Earth is permanent. Weathering and erosion are two powerful forces that work together to slowly chisel, shape, and polish the surface of Earth every second of every day. Weathering breaks down rocks by mechanical and chemical means, while erosion transports the fragments away.

Over time, these forces can leave behind awe inspiring landforms, like pyramidal mountain peaks chiseled by ice and wind. Deep valleys and **alluvial fans** are created as rivers slowly whittle away layers of rock and deposit them as sediment. Cliffs braced against battering waves will eventually topple into the ocean and turn to sand. Regardless of how weak or strong these forces may be, weathering and erosion are constantly building up and tearing down the landscape. If you ever want to see the evidence left behind by weathering and erosion, just go outside and have a look at the different land formations around you. It is guaranteed that you will find something interesting!

 Earth's Varied Geology Explore how weathering and erosion can shape the landscape.

In certain parts of the desert, weathering and erosion caused by sand, wind, and water can sculpt and polish desert formations like **fins, hoodoos, mesas, and buttes**.

Butte

Mesa

Hoodoo   Fin

Sea cliffs and **islands** are battered and slowly eroded away by wind and waves. Weathering and erosion of these cliffs results in some of the sand that accumulates on **beaches** and sand bars. Other coastal features can form, such as **peninsulas**, **isthmuses**, and **coves**.

Cove

Cliff

Isthmus

Island

Peninsula

Stage 3: Soil

What is Soil?

What happens when you put bits and pieces of rocks and minerals, grass clippings, fruit and vegetable trimmings and peels, fallen leaves, twigs, water, oxygen, and a handful of worms in a compost bin? After several weeks, you should end up with a uniform, dark brown, crumbly product with an earthy aroma—soil.

Soil is a loose mixture of weathered and eroded rock particles, organic matter, mineral fragments, water, and air. It covers much of the land surface on Earth. This complex mixture is essential to life on the planet; all living organisms are connected to soil in one way or another. It supports a wide range of organisms—from microorganisms to massive stands of redwoods. In addition, humans depend on soil to provide stability for building structures, grow fruits and vegetables, sustain livestock, and act as a natural water purification system.

What's in Soil?

Have you ever been near a swamp or a bog, visited a farm, planted a tree, hiked up a mountain trail, or played sports on a grassy field? If so, whether you realize it or not, you've come into contact with soil. Cleaning off your shoes or removing dirt stains from your clothes, you may have noticed that soil comes in a variety of colors, textures, smells, and staining abilities.

Organic Material

Soil is an earthy mixture of organic and inorganic matter. Material that was once living is **organic matter**. The majority of the organic matter in soil can be found in the humus. **Humus** contains decomposed plant and animal remains and is a dark-colored substance very similar to what you get from a compost bin. These remains can come from all sorts of places. They come from trees dropping their leaves in the fall, or branches and twigs breaking off during heavy winds. The animal remains in the humus depend on the types of animals that live in the area. Given enough time, all this organic material will decompose to form humus. Humus is important for plant growth because it contains essential nutrients, like nitrogen, sulfur, phosphorus, and potassium. As plants grow, they absorb these nutrients from the soil.

Microorganisms are another organic component of soil. Vast numbers of these microscopic organisms depend on the remains of plants and animals for food. Microorganisms break down and decompose the remains of plants and animals. As microorganisms break down organic matter, they release nutrients, like nitrogen and phosphorus, that make the soil rich and fertile. This greatly contributes to the humus that contains most of the nutrients stored in soil.

Darker layers of soil (dark brown/black) indicate high levels of organic matter whereas lighter layers are generally richer in minerals.

Rowena R/Wikimedia Commons

Inorganic Material

The **inorganic matter** within soil comes from material that was not once living, including rocks and minerals. Weathering and erosion supply much of the inorganic components of soil. As rocks break down into smaller-sized particles, minerals eroded from the rocks are incorporated into the soil. Most inorganic material comes from clays formed from weathered granite and other rocks containing silicate minerals. Soil types differ around the world because the rocks and minerals of these areas differ.

Other common inorganic components of soil include water and oxygen. The amount of water and oxygen stored in soil depends largely upon soil sediment size and texture.

✓ Check for Understanding

Why are microorganisms important for soil formation?

Effects of Grain Size

If you have ever done any gardening, you've probably noticed that not all soil looks or feels the same. Soil varies in texture. Desert soil has a coarse and grainy texture, while the soil located next to a stream bank may have a fine-grained, silky texture. Soil texture depends on the amount of sand, silt, or clay it contains. However, texture is not just about the way a soil feels, it also influences the amount of air, water, and nutrients the soil can hold in its pore spaces.

Team Highlight

The Argos prepare their soil samples in a laboratory at ORNL. They will study the physical characteristics and soil chemistry at Mount St. Helens and in the switchgrass field, including the amount of carbon that accumulated in both locations as the ecosystems recover.

Peter Haydock/The JASON Project

USGS

Fine-Grained Sediment

Soil composed of fine-grained silt or clay sediment has a silky feel to it. Grain size and texture affect the way soil can absorb water, oxygen, and nutrients. Sediment particles within the soil are so tiny and closely packed that there is little space for air between the grains. It can, however, hold a lot of water. During periods of heavy rain, fine-grained soil can become very heavy and water-logged. Unlike soil composed of larger grain sizes, water cannot flow through smaller grained soil as easily and becomes trapped.

Coarse-Grained Sediment

Coarse-grained soils have larger air spaces between grains. The larger grains do not fit together as well and air can be trapped in the pore spaces between grains. These types of soils are often described as being porous. Connected pore spaces make these soils permeable or "leaky," allowing water to pass through quite easily. However, water moving through soil can also dissolve and carry away many of the important nutrients and minerals essential for plant growth.

Some geologic changes may take thousands and even millions of years to make any noticeable difference. However, volcanic eruptions, like the one at Mount St. Helens on May 18, 1980, changed the landscape almost instantly! Before the eruption (L); after the eruption (below).

Influence of Soils

You may have noticed that certain plants only grow in certain environments. For example, a plant that thrives in a swampy environment would not be found living in a dry desert. Areas like swamps or bogs support plants that need soil high in moisture and organic components. On the other hand, plants that have adapted to dry soils require soils that form in deserts. The amount of humus and the ratio of a soil's mixture of small- and large-sized sediment play a significant role in determining the life that an area can support.

When it comes to gardening, the ideal soil is called loam. **Loam** refers to soil that has equal proportions of fine and coarse grains. The smaller fine grains help it retain water and nutrients while the larger coarse grains allow the soil to hold a sufficient amount of oxygen.

✓ Check for Understanding

Explain how grain size determines water, oxygen, and nutrient content.

Soil Formation

The types of soil you may find while gardening in your backyard, hiking along a mountain trail, or fishing off the shore of a lake are different because of how they formed. A combination of factors are responsible for soil formation. These factors include parent material, climate, organisms, location, and time.

Parent Material

Parent material is the main material from which soil is formed. Soil can form from bedrock, organic material, other soil, or deposits from water, wind, glaciers, and volcanoes. The parent material influences the composition of the soil by determining the material it contains.

Climate

Earth has many different climates which can range from the cold arctic of the poles to the hot and humid tropical regions near the Equator. Factors such as temperature, precipitation, and sunlight determine the climate of these regions. These factors also influence weathering and erosion of rocks and minerals, which ultimately affects soil formation.

▲ Loam is an even mix of fine- and coarse-grained sediment.

Living Organisms

Plants require a certain amount of water and nutrients stored in the soil. There is a constant cycle of give and take. Plants extract nutrients from the soil in order to grow. In time, they give the nutrients back in the form of fallen leaves and branches. Plants also provide soil with shade, preventing it from drying out. Plant roots also contribute to soil formation by providing an anchor so that soil does not erode away.

Organisms living in the soil also affect its formation. They help to decompose waste materials within the soil and affect how these materials are distributed. Plant and animal remains on the soil surface are decomposed by microorganisms. This eventually becomes the organic component that makes soil fertile.

Location

The location where soil forms can greatly affect its formation. For example, certain areas are more exposed to weathering processes than others. Soil that directly faces the sun will be dryer than soil that does not. Soil located at the bottom of a hill will get more water than soil that forms on a slope. Soil that forms on a slope can also be lost through erosion.

The accumulation of minerals, vegetation, and animal waste largely depends on the region in which soil forms. Certain locations may have more mineral deposits than others. Plants growing in a certain area will drop their leaves in that area, contributing to a greater amount of humus. Some locations may be more suitable to a type of animal; therefore, waste from that animal will accumulate in those areas, creating humus rich in nutrients.

Time

The most important factor of soil formation is time. It takes time to weather and erode rock. Organisms need time to decompose plant and animal remains.

As time passes, soils tend to mature and deepen. Gradually, the materials that make up a soil develop distinct layers called horizons. A **soil horizon** is a layer of soil that has a different color and texture than the layers above and below it. The combination of the horizons within soil is called a **soil profile**. The soil horizons can change depending on the location of the soil.

✓ **Check for Understanding**

Describe five factors important to soil formation.

Soil Profiles

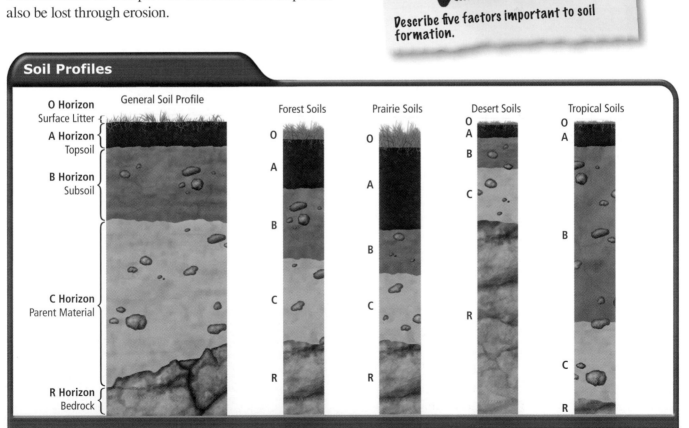

Each soil profile contains horizons, which vary in depth and composition depending upon the factors that contribute to soil formation: parent material, climate, living organisms, location, and time.

Soil Analysis

Perennial grasses and trees are being considered as potential sources of ethanol, a renewable fuel. Dr. Virginia Dale and her team are studying these bioenergy crops to figure out their optimum growth conditions and how they may impact the local environment, including the soil. Their research is showing that the long roots of perennial crops, like switchgrass, may improve soil formation. And, when plant species are grown in their native areas, very few chemical fertilizers need to be added to the soil.

In this activity, you will learn to analyze the physical, chemical, and biological composition of soils in the lab. Then you will collect and analyze soils from your local region to determine factors that may influence the types of plants and animals that may live in and on them.

Materials
- Lab 3 Data Sheet
- balance
- hand lens
- graduated cylinder
- aluminum foil pans
- soil permeability tool (p. 129)
- stopwatch
- soil sieve tool (p. 128)
- funnel
- water
- soil samples provided by instructor
- soil collected in field
- chemical testing strips
- dropper or pipette
- heat lamp
- paper towel
- beakers or cups

Lab Prep

1. Obtain the materials and numbered soil samples from your instructor.

2. Using a hand lens, write a physical description of each sample, including:
   - Color(s)
   - Particle Diversity

3. Use the Soil Mineral Color table in the data sheet to determine the potential mineral composition of each sample.

4. Perform the following tests using the instructions provided in the data sheet.
   - Density
   - Texture
   - Composition
   - Permeability
   - Moisture
   - Organic Content
   - Chemical Analysis

Make Observations

1. Collect a variety of soil samples from your area or school grounds.

2. Briefly describe the area in which each sample was collected. Include information about the types of plants or animals living in and on the soil.

3. Using the techniques in the Lab Prep, analyze each soil sample collected in the field.

4. Share the results of your analysis with your classmates.

5. Compare and contrast each sample with the samples you analyzed during the Lab Prep. Which samples share common properties?

Journal Question What can the analysis of your local soils potentially tell you about the geologic history of your area?

Mark Thiessen/National Geographic Image Collection

Soil Conservation

Many people think soil is "just dirt." However, you should know by now that it is not. Soil is the foundation for all the produce you see in the supermarket. In fact, it is indirectly connected to all the food you had for breakfast, lunch, and dinner. Soil not only affects our food supply, it is also the foundation for the diversity of habitats we share with plants and animals on this planet. It is important that we take care of the soil because however resilient it may appear to be, soil quality is greatly affected by its environment.

▲ This tract of forest has been clear cut. What consequences do you think clear cutting may have on the soil and environment?

Soil Damage and Loss

Soil can be affected by many factors, such as the weathering and erosive effects of climate. Areas where weathering and erosion occur are sometimes caused by building and agricultural practices.

Certain forestry practices, such as clear cutting, are good examples of this. If all the trees growing in a certain area are suddenly harvested, the soil is then left exposed to all the weathering and erosion forces caused by climate. Without the cover of the trees, the sun evaporates the water the soil once stored. Tree roots that once held the soil in place can shrivel up and die leaving the soil vulnerable to erosion by wind and rain. Along with the loss of the nutrient-rich soil, wildlife can also be affected. The quick changes we impose on the environment will more than likely result in drastic consequences.

Forestry Practices

Forestry practices used today have improved. Some companies try to minimize the damage they cause to a habitat by using a variety of techniques depending on the landscape. For example, cut trees can be replaced with seedlings that, over time, will grow and keep the soil healthy. Another technique involves cutting only certain areas of trees within a forest to allow the land to recuperate faster from the damage caused by cutting. Untouched stands of trees are able to provide shelter for disturbed wildlife. Finally, a buffer zone of trees situated around rivers and streams is maintained. This helps prevents erosion of soil and sediment into streams and rivers, which can adversely affect aquatic life.

Farming Practices

Farmers must also consider the effects of their practices. In the past, very little consideration was given to how different crops required different amounts of nutrients from the soil. Farmers soon realized that after just a few planting seasons, extremely fertile soil was exhausted of its nutrients and not able to grow hearty plants.

Farmers today use techniques, like crop rotation, to help keep their soil fertile. For one season, farmers grow a crop, such as corn. After the corn is harvested, they can plant crops of a different family, such as sweet potatoes, or they may not plant anything to let the land lie fallow and rest. After these crops are harvested, farmers plant legumes, such as soy beans or alfalfa. Legumes are a type of plant that grow with the help of a special type of bacteria around their roots. These bacteria, called nitrogen-fixing bacteria, help to replenish the soil with much needed nitrogen.

Tero Laasko/Wikimedia Commons

Chris Johns/National Geographic Image Collection

Another soil conservation technique is the planting of crops specifically grown to provide soil cover. These are called cover crops and prevent erosion by wind and water by covering the soil and holding the soil together with their root systems. Some crops, such as legumes, can also increase soil quality and fertility.

Cover crops suppress the growth of weeds that would otherwise flourish on rich bare soil by taking up the available space and light. They can also control insect infestation by attracting beneficial insects like lady bugs or ground beetles. Insect diversity can prevent pest infestations by bringing populations into balance with a natural predator/prey relationship.

Peter Haydock/The JASON Project

EVEREST

Supercomputers need super display screens. In order to display the massive data sets from science and engineering and biological simulations, and geographic information system (GIS) data, Oak Ridge National Laboratory has built EVEREST (Exploratory Visualization Environment for Research in Science and Technology). This state-of-the-art, super-sized display allows scientists, engineers, and technicians to view and manipulate the data processed by ORNL's supercomputers in ways that a desktop display cannot.

Size: 9.14 m (30 ft) by 2.43 m (8 ft)

Display Panels: Three 2.43 m (8 ft) by 3.05 m (10 ft) optically enhanced glass sections

Projectors: 27 - 2500 lumen projectors

Graphics Rendering: 14 PC nodes connected by a gigabit speed network. Each PC has four dual core processors and high end graphics cards.

Software: Open source, gaming and custom written applications

EVEREST allows researchers in many scientific areas to analyze their data sets in real time. Details that can be lost on smaller screens are very pronounced and become significant when projected. Dr. Virginia Dale uses EVEREST to look at GIS data, such as soil characteristics and ecological niches. She and her team can then identify areas of the country where switchgrass farms might improve soil and water quality, while being close enough to biorefineries to produce an affordable fuel supply.

Farming for Energy Crops

Globally, soil holds twice as much carbon as the atmosphere because of all of the plant material that it contains. Many soils have room to store additional carbon, and getting more carbon into plants and soils is one way that humans might be able to remove some carbon dioxide (CO_2) from the atmosphere, which may help curb global climate change.

Farmers have traditionally tilled their lands to produce crops, but agitating the soil in this way can cause up to half of the carbon trapped in the soil to be released to the air. By converting some farmland to certain grasses or trees that only need to be re-planted every ten years or more, humans may be able to reduce carbon loss from soils while at the same time producing renewable fuels. The deep roots of these perennial energy crops could store more carbon in the soil. There would be other environmental benefits, too. Soils that contain more carbon are able to hold more water and nutrients for crops. Water in the surrounding streams would be cleaner since the stable plant roots would prevent sediments from washing into them on rainy days and since chemical fertilizers would no longer be needed. Less plowing of the land would mean cleaner, dust-free air.

Studying the combined advantages and limitations of growing switchgrass and other energy crops is another area of Dr. Virginia Dale's research. While her work at Mount St. Helens involves looking at changes in an environment over time, her biofuels research involves the study of changes in the environment over space. She seeks to understand where and to what extent land should be converted to energy crops in order to maximize the benefits to our society.

✓ Check for Understanding

How does soil affect your food supply?

Describe some soil conservation strategies.

The Value of Soil

Understanding soil helps us gain valuable knowledge of how ecosystems work. We realize that varying sediment size can alter a soil's ability to hold water and oxygen, and is very important for agriculture. This knowledge helps us ensure that the soil being used has the potential to store sufficient water to keep plants growing through drought and floods and can provide the necessary nutrients for optimal plant growth. Understanding the characteristics of soil also gives us information on how well soils will perform as filters of wastes, as habitat for organisms, and as stable locations for buildings.

Because soil is the product of weathering and erosion, and contains the remains of plants and animals, it provides us with important clues to past geologic events. The more information we have about soil, the better we are able to understand and evaluate the past events that have affected our environment.

✔ Check for Understanding

Describe three ways soil is valuable.

◀ Farmers have hand-carved the steep slopes of Madeira, Portugal into a patchwork of productive farmland. They have done this by building a series of step-like benches, or terraces, supported by either sod or stone walls. These walls work to obstruct the process of erosion by slowing the flow of water that would normally run down the slope.

B. Anthony Stewart/National Geographic Image Collection

Monitoring Soil Changes

Recall that your mission is to *scour Earth's surface for evidence of weathering and erosion – processes that sculpt and shape our ever-changing planet*. Now that you have been fully briefed, you will apply your understanding of weathering, erosion, and soils to help monitor soil quality.

Soil is the foundation for a large proportion of life that exists on this planet. The constant forces of weathering and erosion, as well as land management practices, greatly affect the way soil develops. Dr. Virginia Dale is interested in the factors that may affect soil over space and over time. With the help of a team of scientists, Dr. Dale has been monitoring the carbon content in soil, an indicator of soil fertility and richness, to observe the effects of different management strategies in several different locations.

Josh Morin/The JASON Project

Long term monitoring studies also provide information about how soils can change over time. Dr. Dale has collected data from Mount St. Helens since its eruption, and has monitored the carbon content changes in different locations. The data gained from her studies will provide people with a better understanding of the factors that may result in soil problems in their area. This data will also help scientists develop ways to help manage these issues more effectively into the future.

In this field assignment, you will analyze data collected by Dr. Virginia Dale over space and over time. You will create a graph that will help you compare soil data from several different locations. Once you have analyzed her soil data, you will test one factor that determines the quality of soil in your local area. Through this analysis, you will develop some strategies for monitoring and evaluating soils in your local community.

Materials
- Mission 2 Field Assignment Data Sheet
- graph paper
- local map (print or online)
- soil infiltration tool (p. 129)
- computer with Internet access
- stopwatch

⚠️ **Caution!** You must have the landowner's permission to access any land in your study. Even if your study site is on public land, inform the proper authorities of your intent. Obtain permission before collecting samples at your study sites. Never travel alone. Take a responsible adult with you to your study site.

Objectives:
- Apply graphing skills to compare the carbon content data provided by Dr. Virginia Dale.
- Analyze soil changes over space and over time.
- Identify and assess the soil quality of several different locations in your local area.
- Provide recommendations for further testing and monitoring of soils in your local area.

Field Prep

1 Read about total organic carbon as an indicator of soil quality in the data set.

  a. Outline some relationships carbon has with soil function.

  b. Outline some effects of poor carbon levels in soil.

  c. Outline some ways carbon levels may be improved in soils.

  d. Using the graph, describe the effect of conventional tilling on organic carbon in soils of different depths.

2 Analyze Dr. Dale's data on carbon levels in a variety of soils. Create a graph for Data Set A and Data Set B from the data sheet.

3 What does Data Set A suggest about the soil quality based on the different types of plants over space?

4 Based on Data Set B, how has the carbon content in the soil changed since the Mount St. Helens eruption? Explain.

5 Assuming that carbon levels have changed at a constant rate, what is the rate of carbon content change on Mount St. Helens per year? Per month? Per week? Per day? Why do you think it is useful to know the rate of change?

6 Go to the Mount St. Helens photo gallery to qualitatively analyze how the environment around the blast zone has changed since its eruption on May 18, 1980.

7 What do Data Set B and the photo gallery suggest about what may be causing the changes in soil quality around Mount St. Helens over time?

8 What are some advantages and limitations to studying an area over space (different locations at the same time) and studying an area over time (same location at different times)?

Mission Challenge

1 Read about soil infiltration as another indicator of soil quality in the data sheet.

   a. Outline some factors that may affect the level of soil infiltration.

   b. Outline some relationships soil infiltration has with soil function.

   c. Which is generally better for soil quality, slow infiltration or fast infiltration?

   d. What are some effects slow soil infiltration has on soil quality?

2 Assemble the soil infiltration tool.

3 Identify areas around your school or community to test soils. Plot these locations on a map of the area.

4 At each location:

   a. Write a physical description of the surroundings, including any plants that are growing in the soil. Use plant identification books to help.

   b. Document any signs of weathering and erosion that may be occurring at the location.

   c. Write a physical description of the soil, including color, texture, and particle diversity.

   d. Use the soil infiltration tool and instructions in the data sheet to determine the infiltration time or rate for soils at each location.

5 Share your data with your class.

Mission Debrief

1 Based on the infiltration data, which locations have slow infiltration times/rates? Which locations have fast infiltration times/rates?

2 Based on the physical analysis of the soil, infiltration times/rates, your observation of the ecology that lives on the soil, and any weathering and erosion that may be occurring, which locations may have higher soil quality? Which may have lower soil quality?

3 Considering your data and observations, develop a strategy for monitoring the soil quality of these locations over time. Develop a hypothesis about soil quality changes at each location before conducting your long term research.

Journal Question What are some other ways you could monitor the soils at each research location in your local community? Conduct research to learn about other methods for measuring soil quality besides carbon content and infiltration. How can this analysis be helpful when making decisions and policies about your community?

SUPER BIG...
SUPER FAST...
SUPER POWERFUL...

SUPERCOMPUTERS!

WHAT'S IN A NAME?

Supercomputers are solving some of the most complex and challenging mathematical, scientific, and engineering problems facing humankind. From predicting weather and climate change to determining the best locations for planting fields of switchgrass, the challenges that require supercomputers are amazingly varied. With their names referring to powerful creatures—both real and mythic— Jaguar and Kraken fit the bill.

POWER TO THE MACHINES!

Jaguar and Kraken are currently the first and third fastest computers in the world. You can find them at Oak Ridge National Laboratory in Oak Ridge, Tennessee. With their own air conditioning system and electrical supply, they occupy over 1,115 square meters (12,000 square feet) of floor space and still have plenty of room to grow. They are so big that they consume one-tenth of the power used by the city of Oak Ridge!

HOW FAST AND BIG?

Computational power is measured in flops—FLoating point Operations Per Second. A flop is the ability to do one mathematical operation, with numbers that have decimals, in one second. For example, if you could determine that 2.65 x 3.14 = 8.321 in one second, you would have just done a flop. Currently, Jaguar has the ability to perform 1.75 petaflops, while Kraken can do 0.825 petaflops.

Flops only measure a computer's speed; computer memory is important as well. Jaguar has over 362 terabytes of memory, and 10 petabytes of hard drive space to store data. When you link this with EVEREST, the supercomputer's 9.14 m by 2.43 m (30 ft by 8 ft) visualization screen, it becomes a super-charged, supercomputer experience!

Prefixes for the International System of Units (SI)			
Prefix	Symbol	10^n	Decimal
yotta	Y	10^{24}	1 000 000 000 000 000 000 000 000
zetta	Z	10^{21}	1 000 000 000 000 000 000 000
exa	E	10^{18}	1 000 000 000 000 000 000
peta	P	10^{15}	1 000 000 000 000 000
tera	T	10^{12}	1 000 000 000 000
giga	G	10^9	1 000 000 000
mega	M	10^6	1 000 000
kilo	k	10^3	1 000
hecto	h	10^2	100
deca	da	10^1	10
		10^0	1
deci	d	10^{-1}	0.1
centi	c	10^{-2}	0.01
milli	m	10^{-3}	0.001
micro	µ	10^{-6}	0.000 001
nano	n	10^{-9}	0.000 000 001
pico	p	10^{-12}	0.000 000 000 001
femto	f	10^{-15}	0.000 000 000 000 001
atto	a	10^{-18}	0.000 000 000 000 000 001
zepto	z	10^{-21}	0.000 000 000 000 000 000 001
yocto	y	10^{-24}	0.000 000 000 000 000 000 000 001

JAGUAR AND SWITCHGRASS

With technology improving every day, it is always a challenge to keep up with the top computers in the world. The staff at Oak Ridge National Laboratory works night and day to make this happen, so that researchers around the world can use Jaguar's power to help solve their most complex computational needs.

Dr. Dale and her team at Oak Ridge National Laboratory use Jaguar to determine optimal locations for planting switchgrass, a source for renewable ethanol. She combines information about weather and climate, soil quality, and locations of biorefineries that will make ethanol from switchgrass. All of this information is processed by the computer to make very detailed maps, which include recommended areas where switchgrass should be planted.

Her programs can even take into account which plants may be suited for different parts of the world, and can calculate the cost of transporting harvested plant material to the biorefineries. States, like Tennessee, can then use these maps to help plan where to plant crops, and where to build biorefineries in order to keep transportation costs low.

All of this computational power and complex programming may help replace much of the world's dependence on non-renewable energy sources, like natural gas and oil, with renewable energy sources, like switchgrass and poplar trees. Other scientists use both Jaguar and Kraken to find solutions to their scientific endeavors. What about you? It may sound amazing, but anyone, including you, can propose to use Jaguar to solve complex computational problems.

YOUR TURN

If you could have Jaguar and Kraken complete complex calculations for you, what would you have them do? Brainstorm with your classmates to design a study that would require data collection that could be compiled by Jaguar and Kraken. What would be the focus of your study? What would you need the supercomputers for? Write a proposal to Oak Ridge National Laboratory that describes your proposed research, and justify why they should allow you to use the supercomputers.

Analyzing the Evidence
Dating, Fossils, and Geologic Time

"We face a big challenge involving energy, the environment, and Earth. I hope we can all work together to overcome it, and I hope that I'm part of that effort."

—Dr. George Guthrie
Focus Area Leader, Geosciences
National Energy Technology Laboratory

Dr. George Guthrie

George Guthrie and his team of researchers are exploring the world for geologic locations to store greenhouse gas emissions produced by sources such as power plants.

Meet the Researchers Video
Find out how George uses CT scanners and electron microscopes to examine rocks to determine if they are good candidates for storing carbon within Earth.

Focus Area Leader, Geosciences, NETL

Read more about George online in the JASON Mission Center.

Peter Haydock/The JASON Project

Your Mission...

Unravel the mysteries of Planet Earth using ancient clues and cutting-edge technologies.

To accomplish your mission successfully, you will need to

- Apply different dating methods to calculate the age of Earth.
- Assess the impact of technology on our understanding of Earth's history.
- Examine fossils to investigate how life and environmental conditions have changed over time.
- Analyze rock and fossil evidence to construct a story detailing Earth's past.
- Apply an understanding of Earth's history to help address environmental concerns.

Join the Team

In a secure room on the National Energy Technology Laboratory's campus in Morgantown, WV, Dr. George Guthrie and Argonauts (L to R) Connor Bebb, Maria Marquez, Cindy Duguay, and Emily Judah use an enhanced CT scanner to examine how air and liquids flow through different rocks. The CT scanner has an attachment that can inject different gases and liquids into the rock samples. From this information, George can study the layers of Earth to find the rocks with the greatest potential for sequestering the greenhouse gas carbon dioxide (CO_2).

Man on a Mission

Dr. George Guthrie is on a mission. But rather than fighting dangerous villains, Dr. Guthrie is combatting the emission of carbon dioxide (CO_2) and its effects on Earth's atmosphere. At the National Energy Technology Laboratory in Morgantown, West Virginia, he works to find places to store the massive amounts of CO_2 that humans have poured into the atmosphere. It is a race against time, millions of years in the making.

Over 350 million years ago, the climate of modern day Europe and North America was warmer and wetter than it is today, and CO_2 levels were higher. Massive tracts of swamps formed across these sections of the globe, containing gargantuan trees and dragonflies the size of hawks! As the debris from fallen trees and other plants accumulated, a chemical chain reaction was set in motion. This buried plant matter turned into coal over time and was removed from the natural cycles occurring on the planet's surface.

Humans have been using this coal as a significant energy source for a couple thousand years. At first, changes to the atmosphere from burning coal were only observed locally, as thick columns of smoke. But since the Industrial Revolution, the number of factories and the amounts of emissions released have increased worldwide. Scientists are now concerned that the levels of CO_2 in the atmosphere are growing too quickly. Carbon emissions are having a dire result on our atmosphere and may be contributing to global climate change.

Global reductions in CO_2 emissions may help, but are not the only answer. Where can we put the emissions, instead of allowing them to fill the air? This is no small task—every year, over 33 billion tons of CO_2 are emitted worldwide into the atmosphere due to human activity. That's enough CO_2 to fill approximately 8.3 billion hot air balloons each year! Where could you store all of that? To help solve the problem, Dr. Guthrie has joined a team that is looking for places deep within Earth where carbon can be stored. This literally ground-breaking research will possibly reduce the impact of emissions on the atmosphere, and therefore, the environment.

Erick Ward/Wikimedia Commons

Mission 3 Briefing Video Prepare for your mission by viewing this briefing on your objectives. Learn how George Guthrie and his team use the geologic history of Earth to locate areas where carbon emissions can be stored.

In This Section:

You Will Learn

How old is Earth?
What is relative age?
What is radiometric age?

This is Why

By using different methods to date rocks, scientists can better understand the age of Earth.

Stage 1: The Age of Earth

Developing a Story

When investigators arrive at a crime scene, they quickly sweep the scene for clues. Analyzing these clues will help them begin to develop a story that answers important questions. When did this crime happen? Where did it happen? Who was involved? How did it occur? Guided by these questions and the clues they uncover, investigators can begin to solve a crime that they themselves did not see.

Evidence brought back to the crime lab can be further analyzed using technology, such as computers, to provide investigators with a more detailed story of what happened. As new evidence is found, better leads can be established, allowing investigators to revise their story of what happened. Hopefully, enough information can be gathered to solve the crime and close the case.

So, what do scientists and crime scene investigators have in common? They both use observational skills and technology to analyze clues to create, revise, and understand events that they did not see happen.

Using their observational skills and cutting-edge technology, Dr. Guthrie and his team are working to find suitable underground layers of rock to store carbon dioxide gas released from sources such as fossil fuel power plants. The collection and underground storage of carbon dioxide gas is called **carbon capture and sequestration (CCS)**. Since some rock layers developed over millions of years, Dr. Guthrie and his team must apply their understanding of Earth's history to help locate the best potential sites.

Once a potential site is located, the team must analyze the physical and chemical properties of the layers of rock. They use technology, such as CT scanners, specialized flowmeters, and cutting-edge analytical techniques, to help determine if these rock layers are suitable for the job. If this research is successful, carbon dioxide gas can be stored safely underground instead of being released into the atmosphere, so that we may curb the effects of climate change.

Solving the case of Earth's history is important because of the effects humans can have on our environment. If future CCS sites are to be located, we must further unravel the mysteries of Earth's past.

Today, scientists continue to discover new fossils, rocks, and minerals. These clues are used to revise and further deepen our understanding of Earth's long history. And, as we develop new technologies, we can gain even more information from these clues about our planet's 4.5 billion year history.

Relative Age

How old is Earth? This question is continually debated and revised by scientists. The currently accepted scientific estimate of Earth's age is about 4.5 billion years old. So, how did we arrive at this number?

In the 17th century, Danish scientist Nicolaus Steno spent time observing the different layers of rock that had formed in Tuscany, Italy. The ideas he developed from his observations started a new branch of geology called **stratigraphy** – the study of rock layers. Inspired by observations of rock layers, Steno established the basis for **relative dating**. The concept of relative dating is that layers of rocks are ordered chronologically, so their ages can be compared.

Law of Original Horizontality

Steno developed two laws concerning relative dating. The first was the **Law of Original Horizontality**, which states that all sedimentary rock layers initially form in horizontal layers, and that any change from that horizontal position is due to the rock being disturbed later.

✓ Check for Understanding

Why does Dr. Guthrie need to know about Earth's history to find underground storage locations for carbon dioxide?

James L. Amos/National Geographic Image Collection

Relative Age of Rock Layers

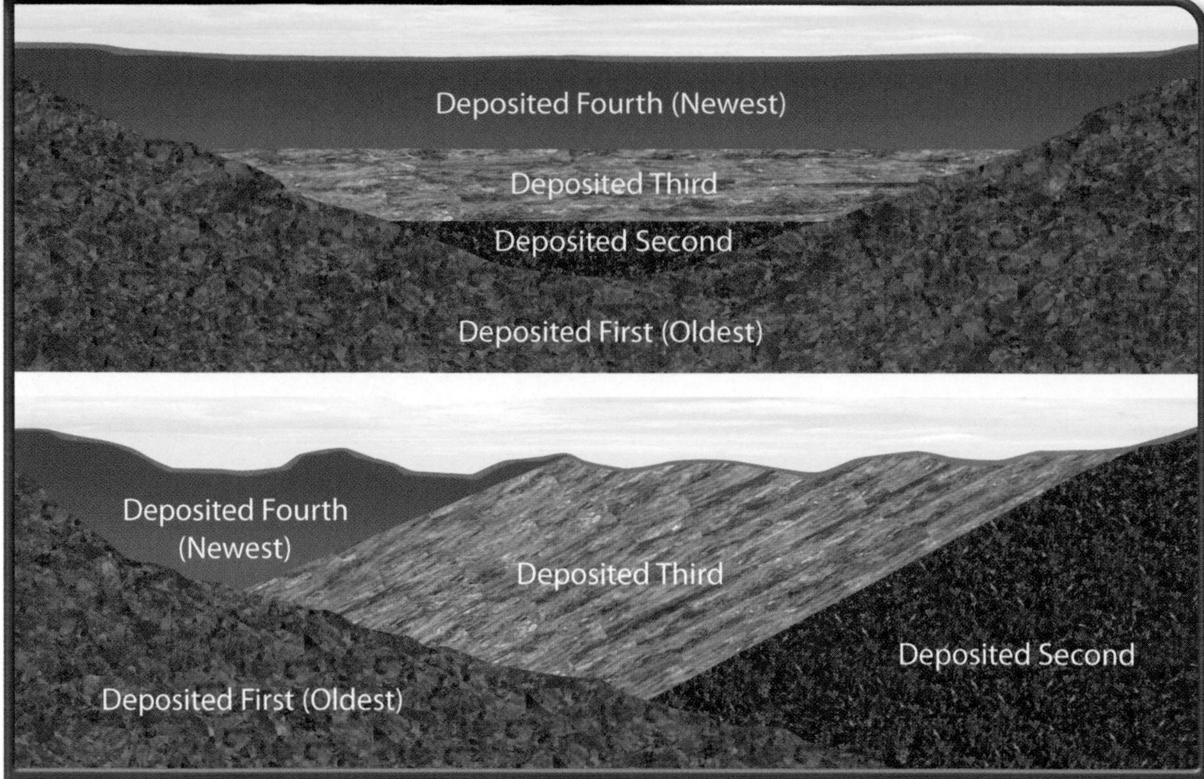

Deposited Fourth (Newest)

Deposited Third

Deposited Second

Deposited First (Oldest)

Deposited Fourth (Newest)

Deposited Third

Deposited Second

Deposited First (Oldest)

Horizontal rock layers can be easily distinguished between oldest and youngest; however, layers can shift as Earth exerts its geologic forces over time.

IFE/COEAO

Explorer's Connection

When Dr. Bob Ballard and his team of explorers discover sunken ships, their job has just begun. They must carefully examine the wreckage for clues that could help piece together ancient events of human history. Armed with state-of-the-art navigation systems, sonar, and the remote operated vehicles Hercules and Argus, one of their latest finds was an ancient 7th century vessel lying 457 m (1,499 ft) below the surface of the Aegean Sea.

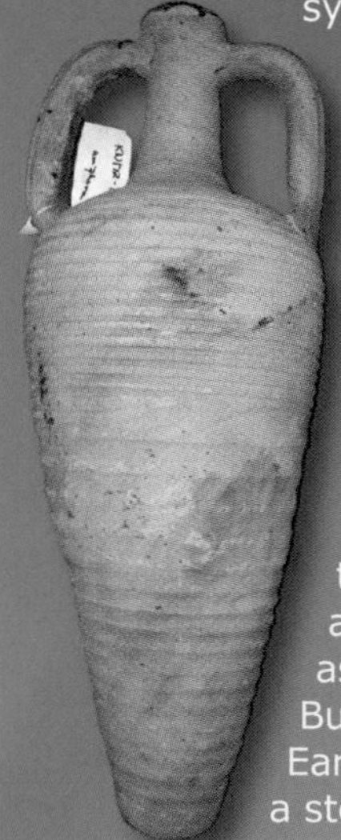

Clues, like the shape of the anchor or style of a ceramic container, were used to help date the ship and describe its purpose. Who knows what Dr. Ballard and his team will find as they investigate the wreck further? Sunken ships are historical treasures and can be as informative as ancient fossils. But, instead of creating a story of Earth's past, they are used to construct a story of human history.

Law of Superposition

Steno then developed the **Law of Superposition** to describe the relative ages of the rock layers in an area. His idea was that, in sedimentary rock layers, the older layers of rock are deposited first. Then, newer, younger layers are deposited and formed on top of these older ones. So, if you observe an undisturbed layer of rock, you can assume that the oldest rocks are at the bottom and the youngest are on the top.

Changing Ideas

Steno's laws revolutionized the way people viewed the age of Earth. In the 1800s, scientists measured the approximate thickness of all sedimentary rock layers at Earth's surface. These measurements ranged from about 25–112 m (15–70 mi). They then observed and measured the rate at which sedimentary layers form, and calculated it to be around 0.3 m (1 ft) every 1,000 years. Using these rates, scientists then calculated how long it would take for all of the sedimentary layers in the world to build up. Based on these calculations, these scientists determined that Earth had to be perhaps a hundred million years old! This was much older than Steno's estimate of a few thousand years.

Math Connection

If layers of sedimentary rock form at a rate of 0.3 meters every 1,000 years, how long would it take to form a 500-meter thick layer of sedimentary rock?

Changing Stratigraphy

Even though estimates of Earth's age were revised to be near 100 million years old, scientists were still underestimating the age of Earth. The revised age did not take into account processes, such as weathering, erosion, and underground geologic activities, that cause change at the surface. These processes are gradual and sometimes are not noticeable for extremely long periods of time. It could take millions of years for weathering and erosion to unearth underground structures. The folding and twisting of rock layers resulting from pressure below may also take millions of years.

For example, geologic forces can exert enough pressure to cause horizontal layers of rock to fold. When the layers fold downwards and form a bowl-like shape, it is called a **syncline**. When the layers of rock fold upward like an arch, it is called an **anticline**. The forces that cause these features can often bring old layers of rock to the surface, where they are exposed to the agents of weathering and erosion.

Over time, parts of the older layers in an anticline can be weathered and eroded away. New, horizontal layers can then form on top of this eroded surface. These gaps in the geologic record, due to layers of rocks lost to weathering and erosion, are called **unconformities**.

▲ An anticline near Bcharre, Lebanon shows a sequence of rock layers that are progressively older toward the center of the fold.

Implications for Carbon Sequestration

The presence of synclines and anticlines do more than make the relative dating of rock layers difficult. To Dr. Guthrie, it also has an impact on a region's suitability to be a carbon sequestration location.

How these syncline or anticline patterns in the rock layers affect a region's suitability for carbon sequestration can vary. On the one hand, the stress caused by pushing layers of rock together can cause cracks in the rock layers. Carbon dioxide gas sequestered below anticline and syncline regions could leak through these cracks, which could make it impractical for the safe storage of carbon dioxide. However, anticlines could create favorable carbon storage sites, because their shapes might act as a container to hold the gas.

▼ The construction of Interstate 68 through Sideling Hill in Maryland exposed ancient layers of rock that folded into a syncline about 330 to 345 million years ago.

Try This!

Make four to six pancake-sized shapes using different colors of clay. Create layers by stacking these shapes on top of each other. Each layer represents a horizontal layer of sedimentary rock. Push the ends of the layers of clay into one another. Using the sharp edge of a ruler, cut down the middle of the stack.

What do the layers look like? Do they form a syncline or an anticline?

This process is similar to what happens in nature as geologic forces exert pressure from both ends of sedimentary rock layers.

Relative Intrusions and Extrusions

Analyzing the positions of rock layers is not the only method geologists use to determine the relative age of rocks. Geologists can also find clues about relative age by examining the location of igneous rock formations.

When molten rock cools and solidifies, it forms igneous rock. Igneous rock usually forms as slabs of giant rock. However, hot molten rock can sometimes pierce through layers of other rock. When this hot molten rock cools and solidifies within the pre-existing rock, it forms an **intrusion**. An intrusion is always younger than the layers of rock that it pierces.

An **extrusion** is also an igneous formation. However, an extrusion forms when lava cools and solidifies on top of older rock formations. In undisturbed areas, extrusions are always younger than the rock layers below them.

▲ This dark-colored igneous rock is an intrusion that cooled and solidified through older rust-colored pegmatite rock in Morefield Mine, Virginia.

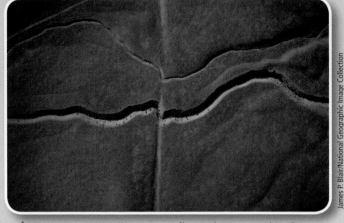

▲ Two streams that once flowed across the San Andreas Fault in Carrizo Plain National Monument, California, have been shifted by geologic forces.

Clues from Faults

A **fault** is a break in Earth's crust usually caused by geologic forces within Earth. These forces move or shift opposite sides of a fault. Faults provide valuable insight into the relative age of rock layers. Since the layer of rock had to be present in order to break, the fault is always younger than the youngest layer of rock cut by the fault.

✓Check for Understanding

Explain why layers of sedimentary rock closer to the surface are usually younger than layers found deeper below Earth's surface.

Why might layers of rock that show syncline and anticline patterns be unsuitable for carbon sequestration?

Lava flowing above pre-existing rock solidifies to form an extrusion. Extrusions are younger than the layers on which they cool and solidify.

Analyzing Core Samples

When assessing potential areas for carbon capture and sequestration, Dr. Guthrie must take core samples to analyze the different layers of rock under the ground at that location. From these core samples, Dr. Guthrie and his team can determine the underground geologic structures they cannot see from the surface. Relative dating techniques can then provide further information to help identify specific layers that may be good candidates for carbon sequestration.

In this activity, your instructor will provide your group or class with rock layers to investigate. Your first challenge is to determine the structure of the rock layers by using only the core samples. Then, from the core samples, you will try to determine the order in which these layers were formed.

Materials
- Lab 1 Data Sheet
- rock layers provided by instructor
- coring tool
- tape
- marker
- ruler

Lab Prep

1. Create your coring tool as indicated by your instructor.

2. Label a grid on your rock layers as outlined in the data sheet. Label the grid with numbers on one side and letters on the other.

3. Identify and document the locations on opposite sides of the rock layers where you will take core samples 1 and 2.

4. Mark these locations on your data sheet.

Make Observations

1. Take core sample 1 by pressing the coring tool straight down and slowly rotating into the rock layers at your predetermined location. Make sure to press and rotate all the way to the bottom.

2. Slowly remove the tool and examine the core. Use a ruler to measure the depth of each layer in millimeters. Record and draw your observations on the data sheet.

3. Remove the core sample from the coring tool and take core sample 2 at the appropriate grid location.

4. Determine which rock layer you think is the oldest, and which is youngest. Why?

5. Based on the core samples, draw a prediction of what the area between the core samples might look like on your data sheet.

6. To verify your prediction, use the coring tool to take two more samples, 3 and 4, locating them between samples 1 and 2. Document your results on the data sheet.

7. Based on the data collected, revise your prediction on your data sheet.

8. Use the coring tool to take two more samples, 5 and 6, within the rock layers. Document your results and revise your prediction as needed.

9. Based on your observations, describe the sequence of events that may have formed these rock layers from oldest to newest.

10. How would increasing the number of core samples taken in the rock layers affect your analysis?

Extension

Gather materials and make your own rock layers. Trade it with another group and try to determine the rock layer structure using the coring tool.

 Journal Question Describe what other information or methods of sampling would help you further develop the sequence of events that created the rock layers.

Radioactivity

When you think of radioactive material, what comes to mind? Glowing green goo? Wild fish-mutant monsters? Maybe radioactive bug-bites that give mild-mannered students super-powers? Fortunately, that is science fiction, not actual science. Real radioactive material is actually in the air you breathe, the food you eat, and in pretty much every single rock on Earth.

Universal Systems HD-350E CT Scanner

CT or "CAT" scanners are usually used in hospitals to look at the internal organs and bones of people. However, on the NETL campus in Morgantown, WV, a CT scanner has been specially modified to look inside rocks. Special drills extract core samples, which are rock samples from deep within Earth—sometimes 1,000 m (3,281 ft) or more. Dr. George Guthrie and his team study the core samples with the CT scanner to look at the spaces inside the rock. Their goal is to find the best rocks that may be used to store carbon dioxide (CO_2), a gas that enhances the greenhouse effect and may be contributing to global warming.

At NETL, the CT scanner has additional equipment attached to it which allows researchers to pump water, CO_2, and methane into the core samples. The scientists study how these fluids flow through the rock. Scientists are looking for rocks that the fluids flow through easily, as well as "cap rocks," or rocks that prevent the fluids from flowing at all. The best underground storage rocks will be very permeable and allow the flow of CO_2, while being capped by a rock that prevents the CO_2 from escaping back to the atmosphere.

Rocks Examined: coal, sandstone, shale

Average Core Size: 4 cm (1.5 in.) diameter and 30 cm (11.8 in.) tall

Largest Core Scanned: 20 cm (7.9 in.) diameter, 152 cm (59.8 in.) long

Rock Tests: rock density and permeability

Fluid Tests: compressibility, velocity, and flow

Resolution: 0.250 mm x 0.250 mm x 2 mm

Time to Scan Each Slice of a Core: 4 seconds

Time to Scan Typical Core: 10 minutes

Number of Scans per Month: 2-3,000

Dual Scanning Energy Levels: 130 kV, 80 kV

CT Control: 1 desktop computer

CT Data Analysis: 2 networked desktop computers

Flow Simulations: 1- 16 networked desktop computers

NETL has recently acquired an even bigger and more powerful CT scanner. They will use it to look at more rock samples and hopefully find the best underground places in the country to store CO_2.

In order for George Guthrie to assign dates to the samples he finds during his research expeditions, he needs to know a little bit about what makes up these rocks, minerals, soils, and other substances.

The Atom

The building blocks of all substances on Earth, including rocks, skyscrapers, lava, and everything in between, are called **atoms**. You cannot see an individual atom because they are so tiny. There are more atoms in the period at the end of this sentence than there are people on this planet. Even though we cannot directly see atoms, we can observe their impact and learn about how they behave. For example, when you fill up a balloon, you cannot see the atoms going into the balloon, but you see the balloon expanding as a result of filling it with atoms.

Protons, Neutrons, and Electrons

Every atom is made of three basic types of particles: protons, neutrons, and electrons. When atoms have the same number of protons, we say that those atoms are the same element. For example, every atom with 79 protons is a gold atom. All atoms with eight protons are oxygen atoms, all atoms with two protons are helium atoms, and so on. The element is determined by the number of protons in an atom.

Isotopes

When two atoms have the same number of protons but different numbers of neutrons, they are called **isotopes**. Scientists refer to isotopes by stating the name of the element and adding their total number of protons and neutrons together. All uranium atoms contain 92 protons. So, uranium with 146 neutrons is called uranium-238 (remember, we add the 92 protons to the 146 neutrons) and uranium with 143 neutrons is called uranium-235.

Radioactive Decay

Some isotopes, such as uranium-235, are unstable. They will naturally release energy over time to become more stable. This natural release of energy is what we call **radioactivity**. The energy release is significant, and can be used to power nuclear power plants and reactors.

Over time, as the unstable isotopes release energy, they slowly decay to form more stable atoms. This is called **radioactive decay**. In the case of uranium-235, it will undergo radioactive decay to form lead-207. The unstable uranium-235 is called the parent isotope, and

Math Connection

Graphing the amount of parent and daughter isotopes that are in a sample versus its half-life will create two exponential curves. When igneous rocks first form, 100 percent of the parent isotope is present. After one half-life has passed, one-half of the parent isotope has decayed into the daughter isotope. After two half-lives, one-fourth of the original parent material remains and three-fourths is the daughter isotope.

How much of the parent isotope remains after five half-lives?

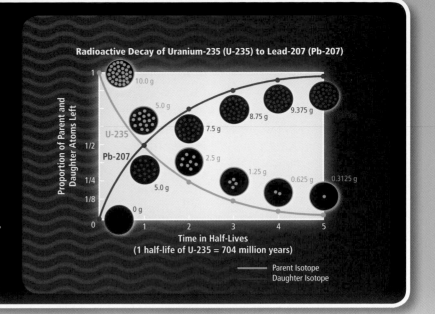

Radioactive Decay of Uranium-235 (U-235) to Lead-207 (Pb-207)

the stable atom it turns into, lead-207, is called the daughter isotope. Luckily, there is a pattern to how isotopes decay. This pattern is the key to understanding why radioactivity is valuable when dating rocks and minerals.

Parent Isotope	Daughter Isotope	Half-Life (years)
Carbon-14	Carbon-12	5,730
Uranium-235	Lead-207	703,800,000
Uranium-238	Lead-206	4,468,000,000
Potassium-40	Argon-40	1,280,000,000
Thorium-232	Lead-208	14,100,000,000

Half-Life

The **half-life** of an isotope is the amount of time it takes for half of the parent isotope to decay into the daughter isotope. For example, imagine you had two kilograms of radioactive uranium-235 (although we would not advise having such a thing). In about 704 million years, one kilogram of the uranium-235 (parent isotope) would undergo radioactive decay to form lead-207 (daughter isotope). After that amount of time, you would have one kilogram of uranium-235 remaining. If you allowed another 704 million years to pass, half of the remaining one kilogram of uranium-235 would decay, leaving you with 0.5 kilograms of uranium-235. Since half of uranium-235 decays about every 704 million years, we refer to 704 million years as the half-life of uranium-235. Scientists use several different isotopes to date rocks, minerals, and fossils because each has a specific half-life.

✓ check for Understanding

Describe the process of radioactive decay.

Determining Radiometric Age

The half-life of an isotope helps scientists determine a rock's **radiometric age**. So how do we take our knowledge of half-lives and use it to date rocks? The process of determining radiometric age is called radiometric dating. To do this, scientists measure the ratio of parent to daughter isotopes in samples collected in the field. Using this ratio, they can determine how many half-lives have occurred since the sample formed. They can then multiply the number of half-lives by the length of time it takes for one half-life to occur.

Both relative and radiometric dating are used by geologists. Relative dating allows geologists in the field to quickly determine when specific layers of rock formed relative to each other. Radiometric dating requires more time and equipment than relative dating. However, this dating technique is more accurate. By examining specific ratios of isotopes in the lab, geologists can estimate the actual age of mountains, fossils, volcanoes, and even Earth!

Math Connection

A rock that contains zircon has a 1 to 3 ratio of U-235 to Pb-207, indicating that two U-235 half-lives have passed. What is the radiometric age of the rock?

(half-lives passed of parent isotope) x (length of time for one half-life of parent isotope) = Radiometric Age

2 x 703,800,000 years = 1,407,600,000 years old

Uranium Dating

Zircon is a mineral that many geologists use to date rocks. The crystal structure of this mineral is especially useful because it contains uranium-235. When zircon originally forms from molten rock, it contains only the parent isotope, uranium-235, and none of the daughter isotope, lead-207. Over time, however, the parent isotope decays into the daughter isotope.

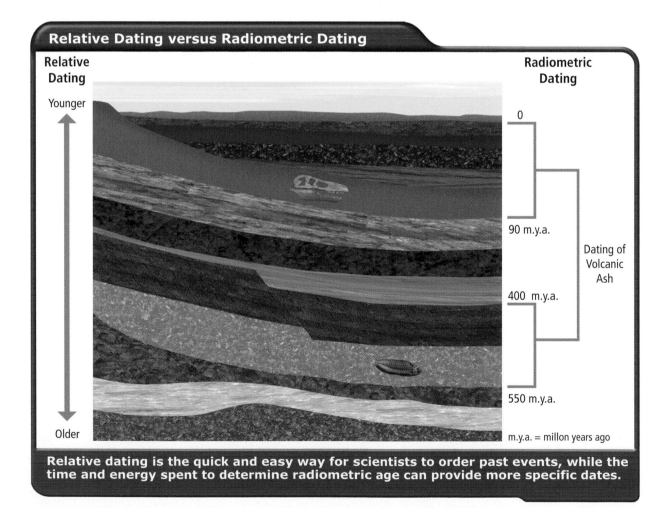

Relative Dating versus Radiometric Dating

Relative Dating

Younger

Older

Radiometric Dating

0

90 m.y.a.

400 m.y.a.

550 m.y.a.

Dating of Volcanic Ash

m.y.a. = millon years ago

Relative dating is the quick and easy way for scientists to order past events, while the time and energy spent to determine radiometric age can provide more specific dates.

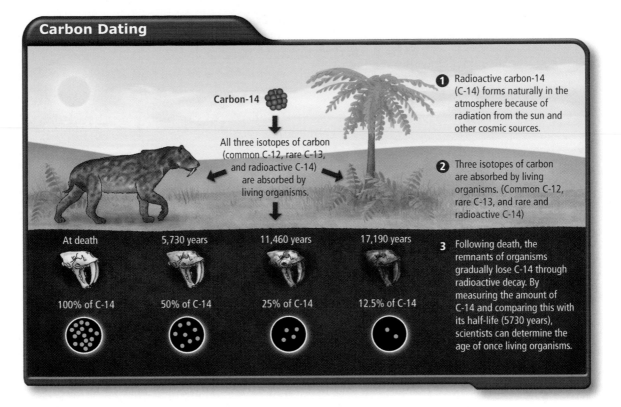

Carbon Dating

Carbon-14

① Radioactive carbon-14 (C-14) forms naturally in the atmosphere because of radiation from the sun and other cosmic sources.

All three isotopes of carbon (common C-12, rare C-13, and radioactive C-14) are absorbed by living organisms.

② Three isotopes of carbon are absorbed by living organisms. (Common C-12, rare C-13, and rare and radioactive C-14)

At death	5,730 years	11,460 years	17,190 years
100% of C-14	50% of C-14	25% of C-14	12.5% of C-14

③ Following death, the remnants of organisms gradually lose C-14 through radioactive decay. By measuring the amount of C-14 and comparing this with its half-life (5730 years), scientists can determine the age of once living organisms.

Carbon Dating

Carbon atoms can be found in the atmosphere as a part of the gas carbon dioxide. Every time you inhale, you take in a small portion of carbon dioxide into your body. A small percentage of this carbon dioxide is carbon-14. Although carbon-14 undergoes radioactive decay to form carbon-12, the amount of carbon-14 atoms within an organism's body remains the same as long as an organism is living.

When an organism dies, it stops taking in new carbon atoms, so the amount of carbon-14 is no longer constant. As time passes, carbon-14 decays to become its daughter isotope, carbon-12, and the ratio between carbon-14 and carbon-12 changes. When scientists discover samples of once living organisms, they can analyze this ratio and calculate the number of carbon-14 half-lives that have passed since its death. Multiplying this number by 5,730 (half-life of carbon-14) will yield the approximate amount of time that has passed since the organism died.

Using carbon to date organisms does have its limitations. Because very little carbon-14 is left over after about nine half-lives, the practical upper limit for carbon dating is about 50,000 years.

Team Highlight

The Argos, along with Dr. George Guthrie, Jamie Brown, and Bill Ayers of NETL, examine different drilling tools. Diamond-coated drill bits, some worth over $10,000, are used to drill to over 1,000 m (3,281 ft) deep to locate layers of rocks that are best for CO_2 storage. This lab uses a machine that simulates the temperatures and pressures the drill bits will encounter to test that the drill bits will perform as expected.

Peter Haydock/
The JASON Project

✓ Check for Understanding

How are isotopes used to determine radiometric age?

Stage 2: Fossils

What are Fossils?

Earth was a very different place long before the appearance of modern day humans. Fascinating creatures, both large and small, swam in the oceans, soared through the skies, and roamed across the lands. This diverse life has never been seen by human eyes. So, how do we know that these creatures ever existed?

Fossils are clues that we use to explore this mysterious past. Fossils are the remains or traces of living organisms preserved in Earth's crust. Fossils can provide us with valuable answers to questions such as: How did these organisms live and why are they not around today?

These are just some of the questions that have inspired people to study paleontology. **Paleontology** is the study of the history of life on Earth. Some of the clues that paleontologists use to explore this fascinating world of the past are fossils found in rocks.

Today, paleontologists apply the same technologies that are used to determine the age of rocks on Earth to fossils. Radiometric dating of fossils has helped scientists explain the existence of once mysterious creatures. These fossils have been dated back to when they once lived.

Fossils continue to be discovered today. In 2006, Norwegian paleontologists found the fossil of a massive carnivorous sea creature that was 15 meters (49 feet) long and had teeth that were 30 cm (12 in.) long! After analyzing its body structure and applying radiometric dating to its remains, paleontologists believe that this creature lived some 150 million years ago.

As new fossils are discovered and dated, scientists understand more about how life and the environment has changed over time. Using tools, like chisels, hammers, maps, and relative and radiometric dating techniques, paleontologists can gather information that helps explain the appearance and extinction of, and even interactions between, prehistoric plants and animals. As technology improves, we can build a better picture of the fascinating world of life that existed thousands, millions, and even billions of years ago.

Fossil Formation Conditions

Most fossils are formed from the remains of an animal's shell or bones, or a plant's woody stem or seeds. Almost instantly after an animal or plant dies, the process of **decomposition**, or rotting, begins. Soft tissue, like leaves, skin, muscles, and organs, begins to decompose first. This is followed by harder tissue, like bones, shells, woody stems, or seeds. If conditions exist where decomposition is slow to set in, over time, an organism may eventually become fossilized instead of fully decomposing.

Factors Affecting Decomposition

Decomposition occurs when microscopic organisms, or microbes, break down plant and animal remains. Microbes secrete specialized enzymes that help them feed upon and break down organic matter. Certain factors affect the way these microbes work, including temperature, humidity, and oxygen.

The enzymes that microbes use to decompose organic tissue work most efficiently in environments that are approximately 40°C (104°F). Temperatures higher or lower than this can slow decomposition.

Humidity levels also affect microbes. Higher humidity levels speed up decomposition because many microbes need moisture to grow and multiply.

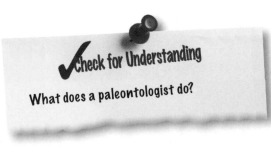

✓ Check for Understanding

What does a paleontologist do?

Sheep81/Wikimedia Commons

Decomposition is also affected by oxygen. Microbes, like humans, need oxygen to live. Without oxygen, most microbes cannot survive, and therefore, decomposition will stop. Levels of oxygen are low in lake bottoms, tree resin, and tar pits, making them ideal environments for fossil formation.

The environment where a plant or animal dies plays a role in fossil formation. If they die in an environment that is not favorable for microbes, there is a better chance that they might be preserved long enough to become fossils.

Rock Types for Fossil Formation

The majority of fossils are found in sedimentary rocks. These rocks are formed by the gradual accumulation and lithification of sediment. Sediment carried by rivers and streams is deposited and builds up when it reaches deeper basins, such as lakes. If an organism dies near these areas of deposition and is covered by sediment before it fully decomposes, it can become part of the sedimentary layer.

Fossils are rarely formed in igneous rocks. These rocks form directly from hot molten rock so there is very little chance that an organism's remains will be preserved under such extreme temperatures.

Fast Fact
Coal deposits are fossilized remnants of entire forests, usually dating back to 300 million years ago. As coal formed, the original plant material was compressed to less than one hundredth of its original size. That means a tree that once stood 60 m (196.8 ft) tall might be compressed to only 60 cm (23.6 in.)!

James P. Blair/National Geographic Image Collection

Metamorphic rocks form from pre-existing rock. The transformation from one rock type to another usually requires high temperature or pressure, or mineral replacement by chemically active fluids. These conditions usually destroy or deform fossils.

✓ Check for Understanding

Why are most fossils found in sedimentary rocks?

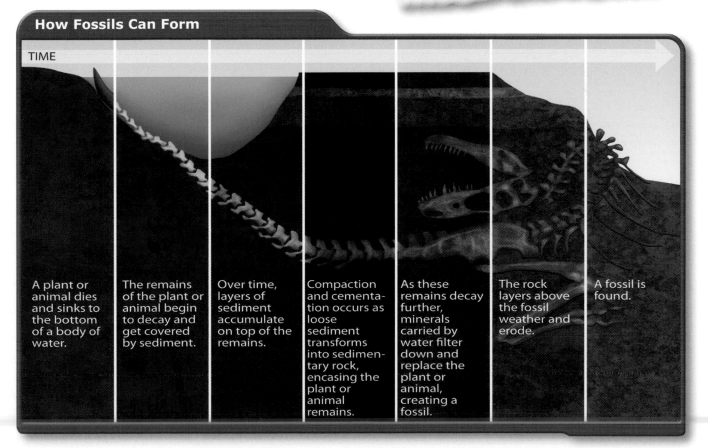

How Fossils Can Form

TIME

| A plant or animal dies and sinks to the bottom of a body of water. | The remains of the plant or animal begin to decay and get covered by sediment. | Over time, layers of sediment accumulate on top of the remains. | Compaction and cementation occurs as loose sediment transforms into sedimentary rock, encasing the plant or animal remains. | As these remains decay further, minerals carried by water filter down and replace the plant or animal, creating a fossil. | The rock layers above the fossil weather and erode. | A fossil is found. |

Learning from Different Fossil Types

Fossils can be classified by how they are formed. Each type helps us learn what life and environmental conditions were like at the time the fossil was formed on Earth.

Arpingstone/Wikimedia Commons

Mold and Cast Fossils

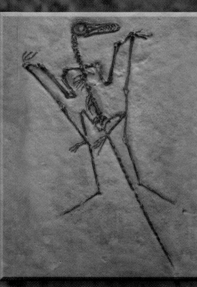

The most common type of fossils forms when a plant or animal dies in a watery environment and is buried under layers of mud and silt. Over time, mud and silt become sedimentary rock that forms around what is left of the plant or animal. Eventually, the buried organism decays or dissolves into solution and is carried away, leaving behind a hollow impression called a **mold**. Mineral-enriched groundwater and sediment can seep into the mold and harden. This results in a replica of the original organism, called a **cast**. Mold and cast fossils preserve an organism's three-dimensional external structures. Paleontologists can examine the surface texture and shape of extinct organisms using mold and cast fossils.

Kevin Walsh/Wikimedia Commons

Mineral Replacement Fossils

Mineral replacement fossils are similar to mold and cast fossils. However, instead of mineral-enriched groundwater filling up and hardening within a mold, the mineral-enriched solution actually soaks into the microscopic spaces found within bones, shells, teeth, or woody plant tissue. Over time, minerals in the solution crystallize within the spaces, preserving the shape of the organism like a statue. Petrified wood is an example of a mineral replacement fossil. A tree covered by sediment was preserved, and minerals dissolved in groundwater seeped into the tree's cells. Over time, the minerals crystallized, filling in all the spaces and creating a fossil.

Robert Sisson/National Geographic Image Collection

Preserved Remains

Some organisms are fossilized in amber, ice, or tar, looking exactly the way they did when they were alive. Amber is the solidified resin of conifers, or evergreens. Resin is secreted by trees as a defense mechanism against insects. It is thick and sticky, and can trap insects and larger animals, such as lizards and frogs. Once trapped, more resin can flow over top, encasing and preserving them perfectly for millions of years. Freezing can also preserve animals and plant remains for a long time. Though the wooly mammoth has been extinct for about 4,000 years, the **preserved remains** of the large herbivore can still be found in Siberian glaciers. Other fossils have been found in tar pits. Organisms trapped in this sticky oil were preserved as tar soaked into their bones, preventing decay.

Anders L. Dansgaard/Wikimedia Commons

Trace Fossils

Trace fossils are the preserved evidence of the activities of once living organisms. Trace fossils can include footprints, trails, dwelling structures, and even preserved fecal material. We can learn about an animal's approximate size and how they walked or ran from trace fossils. They can also provide answers to whether animals lived in packs or alone. Trace fossils can indicate the nesting habits of animals, where the animals traveled, and what the animals ate.

Daderot/Wikimedia Commons

Carbon Film Fossils

Carbon film fossils allow us to observe the softer tissue of plants and animals. They form when an organism is quickly buried by fine clay or silt sediment. Over time, the organism is compressed, and the organic material of the plant or animal is released as gas. This process leaves a carbon-rich film imprinted between layers of rock, and often retains the form of the original organic tissue. These fossils are often found in deposits of shale or mudstone. The analysis of the soft tissue of ancient life helps paleontologists compare details of the fossilized remains with other organisms. For example, the vein patterns in leaves and the detailed structures of insect wings can be compared with those of plants and animals that are living today.

Woudloper/Wikimedia Commons

Fast Fact

Petrified wood can be found strewn across the desert landscape of northern Arizona in almost all of the colors of the rainbow. The presence of petrified wood usually indicates that the area was once buried under a sea of mud, sand, or volcanic ash.

The Fossil Record

Radiometric dating technology has allowed scientists to further analyze already discovered fossils. Documented fossils can be given a radiometric age and then ordered chronologically. This gives scientists a chronologically dated record of many different life forms that existed in the past, called the **fossil record**.

Development of Life

Studying the fossil record shows how life on Earth has developed. It has shown that simple, single-celled organisms, like bacteria, were more prevalent in ancient rocks that date back hundreds of millions of years ago. Younger, more recent rocks contain more complex fossilized organisms, such as flowering plants and primates. This evidence supports the theory that life on Earth has slowly developed from simple, single-cell organisms to more complex organisms, including the plants and animals we see today.

Appearance and Disappearance of Life

By noting the appearance and disappearance of species, the fossil record can provide valuable information about the length of time certain species existed on the planet. For example, we have found dinosaur fossils dating back to about 230 million years ago, but have not found any after around 66 million years ago in the fossil record. From this information, paleontologists have hypothesized when and how long certain dinosaurs lived on this planet. They have also correlated this information with environmental conditions to provide plausible explanations about their extinction.

Using Fossils to Date Rocks

When it is not possible to perform radiometric dating on a rock, scientists can estimate its age by searching for certain organisms fossilized within the rock layers. These fossils have been previously dated by other scientists and are called **index fossils**.

If an index fossil is found within a layer of rock, scientists will have a good estimate of when that layer of sediment was deposited to form the rock.

What makes a good index fossil? Ideally, these fossils were ancient organisms that were fairly common and easily fossilized. Most index fossils are organisms with a hard shell, because they do not decompose as quickly as soft tissue. Index fossils often have distinctive features that allow them to be easily distinguished from closely-related organisms.

Fossilized organisms that spanned a large geographic range are especially useful as index fossils because they allow the relative age of rocks to be correlated over a wide region. Finally, organisms that existed during a short time period, about several million years, are more useful than those that spanned large expanses of time. Shorter geologic durations allow for a more refined relative date.

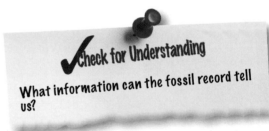

✔ Check for Understanding

What information can the fossil record tell us?

▲ Further investigation of this unspecified fossil from Dinosaur National Monument in Utah will help scientists learn more about this ancient creature that once roamed the land.

Fossil Formation

When Dr. George Guthrie is exploring areas for potential carbon sequestration, he takes core samples to analyze the geologic layers. Fossils are often found within the core samples and layers he examines. But, many times the entire organism is not fully fossilized. Dr. Guthrie and his team must use a variety of techniques to hypothesize about what the missing parts look like from observations of other fossils or plants and animals that are still alive today.

In this activity, you will analyze the effect of sediment composition on the quality of a model fossil. Then, you will use analytical techniques to hypothesize about an organism from a fossil.

Materials

- Lab 2 Data Sheet
- 4 paper cups
- plaster of paris
- clay
- vegetable oil
- tablespoon
- shell or other item with detail
- hand lens
- tape measure
- graph paper
- marker

Lab Prep

1. Label the paper cups A, B, C, and D.

2. Mold a piece of clay for each cup that is slightly smaller than the circumference of the cup and around 1–1.5 cm thick.

3. Press the same surface of a shell or other item into the surface of each clay piece. Gently remove the shell.

4. Gently rub a small amount of oil on the impression in the clay surface. Place each clay piece into the bottom of the cups with the impression facing up.

5. Cover the clay in each cup completely with a mixture of plaster of paris and water, using the following proportions. Allow all mixtures to dry overnight.

Container	Plaster of Paris	Water
A	4 Tbsp	0 Tbsp
B	3 Tbsp	1 Tbsp
C	2 Tbsp	2 Tbsp
D	1 Tbsp	3 Tbsp

6. Remove the plaster and clay from each cup, and gently peel the clay from the plaster fossil.

Make Observations

1. Looking at each plaster fossil, which mixture produced fossilized prints with the most and least detail?

2. Describe some relationships between composition of the sediment and quality of the fossil print in each piece of plaster.

3. Which type of fossil do your plaster fossils most represent, and how do these types of fossils typically form?

4. Your teacher will provide your class with a "fossilized" hand print.

    a. Measure the hand span (distance from tip of thumb to tip of pinky finger).

    b. Describe any distinguishing features on the surface of the hand or fingers.

    c. Knowing how tall you are and the size of your own hand, predict the height of the person who made the print.

5. Use the following method to determine the person's approximate height.

    a. Measure the height and hand span of each member of your group.

    b. Compile the data from the entire class.

    c. Construct a scatterplot of the data where the x-axis is the hand span, and the y-axis is the student's height.

    d. Draw a line of best fit on your graph, and use it to determine the approximate height of the person who made the fossilized print.

6. How do your predictions in steps 4 and 5 compare? How can paleontologists determine information, such as behavior or size, about an animal from fossilized prints, such as dinosaur tracks?

 Journal Question Describe some characteristics of an organism that may make it more suitable for fossilization, and what effect this may have on our understanding of Earth's past.

In This Section:
You Will Learn

What is geologic time?

How is geologic time divided?

What major events happened in the past?

This is Why

By applying an understanding of fossils and the dating of rocks, we can construct a timeline that details events of Earth's past.

Stage 3: Earth's History

Geologic Time

The average lifespan of a human being takes up a miniscule fraction of time in comparison to Earth's overall history. If we were to squeeze Earth's entire 4.5 billion year history into just one year, how much time do you think it took before humans first appeared on this planet?

If Earth formed at exactly 12:01 a.m., January 1, the only signs of life present in the first half of the year would be microscopic, single-celled organisms first appearing near the end of March and living exclusively in the ocean. The development of more complex life, such as hard-shelled mollusks, would not occur until about November 17. On November 20, we would see early forms of fish.

The last week in November would mark the emergence of land plants, along with early ancestors of spiders and scorpions. Amphibians would venture out from the water and inhabit the land starting on December 1. Early reptiles would appear six days later, and dinosaurs would roam Earth from December 12 until late December 25. Early mammals would begin to develop around December 15 and flowering plants would begin to flourish after December 20.

We would need to wait until the evening of December 30—almost an entire year after the formation of the planet—for the emergence of modern humans. That would bring us to "today," which coincides with midnight, December 31.

Major Subdivisions of Geologic Time

Based on the previous time scale, you should better understand the age of Earth. However, from a geologist's point of view, it would be impractical to squeeze Earth's entire history into just one year. Instead of looking at time based on a scale of days and months, they use another method to divide **geologic time**.

Scientists have divided Earth's history into major subdivisions called eons, eras, periods and epochs. These time frames are generally based upon the geologic land formations and organisms inhabiting Earth. They are continually revised as scientists learn new things about Earth's past. Continual improvements in the field of radiometric dating have also improved the accuracy of some of the time estimates for geologic land formations and fossil discoveries upon which these subdivisions are based.

Team Highlight

The Argos collect samples of rocks from an exposed coal seam on the NETL campus to compare with samples taken from inside the mine.

Peter Haydock/The JASON Project

Eons

Eons are the largest division of geologic time. Four eons divide Earth's entire history: the Hadean, Archaean, Proterozoic, and Phanerozoic eons.

The Hadean (formation of Earth – 3,800 million years ago), Archaean (3,800 – 2,500 m.y.a.), and Proterozoic (2,500 – 542 m.y.a.) eons are collectively known as **Precambrian time**. These eons span from the formation of the planet, development of early oceans, the first sedimentary rocks, and the first signs of life. During the late Archaean and early Proterozoic eons, scientists speculate that one of the most important events in biological history took place—single-celled photosynthetic organisms emerged and filled the atmosphere with oxygen.

Roy Anderson/National Geographic Image Collection

The oxygen-enriched atmosphere ushered in new forms of life on Earth. The beginning of the Phanerozoic eon coincides with the appearance of animals with external skeletons. The Phanerozoic eon dates from 542 million years ago to the present. Although it makes up less than 15 percent of Earth's entire history, it represents the time during which the majority of life on Earth has existed.

Eras

The Phanerozoic eon is divided into the Paleozoic, Mesozoic, and Cenozoic **eras**. In general, each era is based upon the group of animals that dominated life on Earth during the time period. This is determined by the prevalence of fossils found dating back to those eras. To that end, the Paleozoic era is called the "Age of Fishes," the Mesozoic era represents the "Age of Dinosaurs," and the Cenozoic is called the "Age of Mammals."

Periods and Epochs

Eras are further divided into **periods**. Periods are partly based upon rock evidence of major disturbances that occurred in Earth's crust. There are 11 periods that divide the eras in the Phanerozoic eon. Periods are further divided into **epochs**.

Piecing Together Time

By applying an understanding of geologic processes and analyzing data collected from radiometric dating, scientists have calculated the age of Earth to be about 4.5 billion years old. Relative and radiometric dating of land formations have provided geologists with an estimated time scale for geologic changes on Earth's surface. The discovery, analysis, and dating of fossils have provided us with estimated time periods for when these prehistoric plants and animals existed.

Scientists have now begun to piece together these clues to create a detailed story of Earth's past. This story incorporates the geologic changes on Earth's surface with the way life has developed since the formation of the planet.

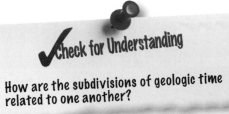

Check for Understanding

How are the subdivisions of geologic time related to one another?

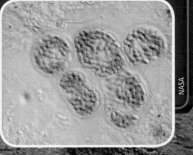
Ruth Ellison/Wikimedia Commons

Hadean, Archaean and Proterozoic Eons (4,500 - 542 m.y.a.)

Formation of a Planet

Scientists believe that earlier than 4.5 billion years ago, Earth was a lifeless ball of swirling dust, rock, and ice revolving around our young sun. The gravity generated by this ball of material attracted other space debris, causing our planet to grow. As Earth grew in size, so did its gravity.

Scientists hypothesize that everything changed when a giant cosmic body collided with Earth. The heat generated from this massive collision melted the entire planet, and the blast caused chunks of molten rock to catapult into space, forming our moon.

Earth's Surface Forms

After this collision, Earth was hot molten rock. As the planet orbited the sun, dense material sank toward the center of the planet, forming Earth's dense metal core. Earth's surface cooled and became solid.

Even though Earth was now solid, the next 700 million years were not hospitable to life. The fumes generated from the cooling rocks on Earth filled the early atmosphere with water vapor and noxious carbon dioxide and nitrogen gases.

Eventually, temperatures dropped and atmospheric gases condensed into droplets of water. Storms followed, raining down and filling empty depressions and basins on our planet's surface to form lakes and oceans.

Life Develops

Approximately 3.8 billion years ago, the impact from comets began to subside. This enabled water to settle on Earth's surface, and the oceans were formed.

At that time, chemical interactions may have produced molecules complex enough to reproduce. These molecules would soon evolve to become more and more complex, similar to certain types of bacteria we see today. These organisms flourished in the sunlit portions of the ocean and, by the trillions, they transformed Earth by filling the atmosphere with breathable air.

Stjepo/Wikimedia Commons

Phanerozoic Eon

Paleozoic Era (542 - 251 m.y.a.)

Cambrian Period (542 - 488.3 m.y.a.)

During the Cambrian period, shallow seas covered much of the land and ancient continents were situated south of the Equator. There was a great explosion of invertebrate life developing in these early seas, including trilobites and mollusks.

Ordovician Period (488.3 - 443.7 m.y.a.)

A warm, shallow sea covered much of Earth. Life was dominated by invertebrates, or animals without internal skeletons. Fossil records indicate that early vertebrates started to appear, including jawless fish.

Kam Mak/National Geographic Image Collection

Silurian Period (443.7 - 416 m.y.a.)

In the Silurian period, coral reefs began to develop. The long, drawn out collisions between moving continents began to form mountains. Fish developed jaws, and plants and arthropods appeared on land.

Devonian Period (416 - 359.2 m.y.a.)

This period marks the "Age of Fishes," as the fossil record shows an abundance of shark and fish fossils. Trilobites and corals were common in the oceans and the first amphibians set foot on land.

Sally J. Bersusen/National Geographic Image Collection

Carboniferous Period (359.2 - 299 m.y.a.)

Plants dominated the landscape in great swamp forests filled with massive woody trees. Most of the coal we burn today is the fossilized remnants of trees from this period. True reptiles appeared, as did winged insects, including dragonflies and cockroaches. **Pangaea**, an ancient super-continent that included all of the major landmasses on Earth, began its formation at the end of the Carboniferous period.

Permian Period (299 - 251 m.y.a.)

The land was dominated by reptiles. Fossil records indicate the largest mass extinction in Earth's history occurred in this period—an estimated 90 percent of marine species and 70 percent of land animals went extinct. Scientists speculate that either large scale climate changes or a series of massive volcanic eruptions caused this mass extinction.

John Sibbick/National Geographic Image Collection

Mesozoic Era (251 - 65.5 m.y.a.)

Triassic Period (251 - 199.6 m.y.a.)

The Mesozoic era is divided into three periods. The early Mesozoic era is called the "Age of Reptiles" and begins the Triassic period. During this period, the central region of Pangaea was dominated by a hot, dry climate. The Triassic period marks the appearance of the first dinosaurs. Early ancestors of present day turtles and crocodiles, as well as the first mammals, also started to appear in the fossil record. Fossils dating to this period indicate that forests consisted mainly of conifers, palm-like trees, and ginkgo trees.

Jurassic Period (199.6 - 145.5 m.y.a.)

Pangaea started its separation during the late Triassic and early Jurassic periods. North America began to separate from Africa and South America. Large dinosaur fossils have been found dating back to this period, including Stegosaurus, Diplodocus, and Apatosaurus. The fossil record also indicates the appearance of early birds.

Cretaceous Period (145.5 - 65.5 m.y.a.)

During this period, continents moved closer to their current positions, with South America splitting from Africa. Geologic evidence dating back to this period also indicates that there was widespread volcanic activity. Flowering plants and snakes appeared. Mass extinctions appear to have been prevalent near the end of this period. Fossil records indicate the sudden disappearance of many land and marine life forms, including the dinosaurs.

Cenozoic Era (65.5 m.y.a. - present)

Paleogene Period (65.5 - 23.03 m.y.a.)

The Cenozoic era is divided up between the Paleogene period and the Neogene period. The Himalayas formed in the Paleogene period. A continental glacier covered much of Antarctica, and continents continued to slowly move to their present day positions. The beginning of this era also marks the "Age of Mammals," when horses, elephants, bears, rodents, primates, and whales began to appear.

Neogene Period (23.03 m.y.a. - present)

The Neogene period began with much of the land covered by a thick sheet of ice. During the last two million years, mammals, flowering plants, and insects have dominated the land. Most scientists speculate that modern humans developed approximately 190,000 years ago in Africa.

Today

Looking at images of Earth from space, it is hard to imagine that this blue and green planet was once a lifeless ball of molten rock. It has taken over 4.5 billion years for Earth to become what it is today.

Dr. George Guthrie is working to apply our current understanding of Earth's history and his own stratigraphy research to provide a means for storing carbon dioxide within Earth. As technology improves and new fossils are unearthed, our understanding of Earth's past will continue to deepen.

Armed with knowledge, skills, and technology, it will be up to young scientists, like you, to further develop this understanding. This will ultimately help us better prepare ourselves for environmental challenges that lie ahead for this ever-changing planet.

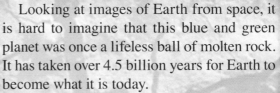

✔ Check for Understanding

Describe some of the developments on Earth that define the change from one period to another.

Spiraling Through Geologic Time

Can you imagine living to be 80 years old or more? Think about everything you can accomplish in a lifetime. Now, imagine the events that can happen over a thousand years, a million years, or even a billion years. Within Earth's 4.5 billion year history, the amount of time humans have existed–approximately 190,000 years–is just a tiny part, and the lifetime of a human–80 years–doesn't even register! Visualizing time isn't easy, but what would it look like if you could see Earth's history unfold before you on a timeline?

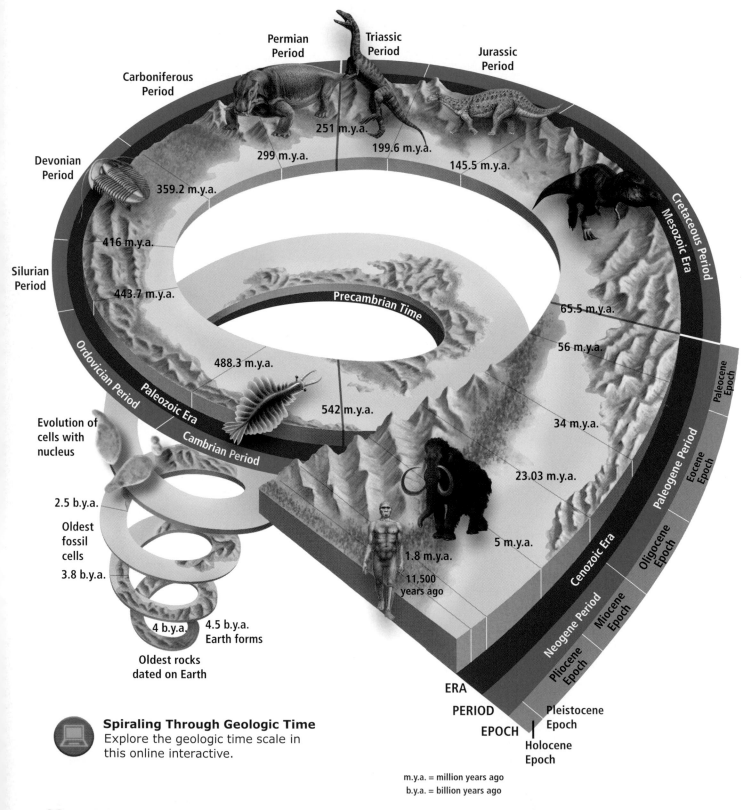

Carboniferous Period
Permian Period
Triassic Period
Jurassic Period
251 m.y.a.
299 m.y.a.
199.6 m.y.a.
145.5 m.y.a.
Devonian Period
359.2 m.y.a.
Cretaceous Period
Mesozoic Era
416 m.y.a.
Silurian Period
443.7 m.y.a.
Precambrian Time
65.5 m.y.a.
56 m.y.a.
Ordovician Period
488.3 m.y.a.
Paleocene Epoch
Paleozoic Era
Evolution of cells with nucleus
542 m.y.a.
34 m.y.a.
Paleogene Period
Eocene Epoch
Cambrian Period
23.03 m.y.a.
Oligocene Epoch
2.5 b.y.a.
Oldest fossil cells
5 m.y.a.
Cenozoic Era
3.8 b.y.a.
1.8 m.y.a.
Neogene Period
Miocene Epoch
11,500 years ago
4 b.y.a.
4.5 b.y.a. Earth forms
Pliocene Epoch
Oldest rocks dated on Earth
ERA
PERIOD
Pleistocene Epoch
EPOCH
Holocene Epoch

Spiraling Through Geologic Time
Explore the geologic time scale in this online interactive.

m.y.a. = million years ago
b.y.a. = billion years ago

Exploring Earth's Past

To help narrow his search for locations for carbon sequestration, Dr. George Guthrie analyzes the geologic history and events which produce rocks that are good for holding carbon. By understanding these processes and history, he can search for new locations that have undergone a similar series of events in their geologic past.

In this activity, you will analyze the geologic history of Earth. To do this, you will build a time scale which includes major events in the geologic past. Using radiometric dating techniques, you will organize these events to gain a better understanding about how Earth has changed over the past 4.5 billion years.

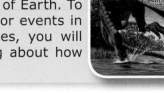

Materials
- **Lab 3 Data Sheet**
- **string**
- **ruler**
- **meter stick**
- **paper clips**
- **tape**

Lab Prep

1. Measure out a piece of string 5 meters long. Tape the string horizontally to a wall.

2. Mark the two ends and every ½ meter along the string with tape.

3. Label one end of the string "Today" and the other end "5 billion years ago."

4. Starting from the side labeled "Today," move to the next piece of tape and mark it "500 million years ago." Move to the next one and mark it "1 billion years ago," the next "1.5 billion years ago," "2 billion years ago," "2.5 billion years ago," and so on until you get to the end marked "5 billion years ago."

5. Based on the setup, what is the scale of the string related to years? (1 m = x Years; 1 cm = x Years)

6. Cut out the Geologic Event cards provided in the data sheet.

Make Observations

1. With your group, determine where you think each card belongs along the time scale. Use a paperclip to attach each card.

2. Document the placement of each card on your data sheet. Provide rationale for the order your group selected. Compare and contrast your order with other groups in your class.

3. Using the radiometric data and the directions in the data sheet, determine the radiometric age of each event.

4. Using this analysis, a meter stick, and the scale, position each event at its appropriate position along the string.

5. How did your original positioning of the events compare to the position based on the radiometric dating?

6. Describe some observations of the distribution of the events on the time scale.

7. Using the dates from the text, mark the beginning and end of each era and period on your string.

8. Based on your time scale, describe some of the changes that may have occurred throughout each era and period of Earth's history.

 Journal Question How would increasing the number of events on your timeline affect your understanding of Earth's geologic past?

Finding Carbon Sinks

Recall that your mission is *to unravel the mysteries of Planet Earth using ancient clues and cutting-edge technologies*. Now that you have been fully briefed, it is time to interpret geologic rock layers to look for potential carbon sequestration sites, or sinks.

Dr. Guthrie is trying to determine and implement technology and infrastructure which promotes carbon capture and sequestration in different geologic regions of North America. To do this, Phase I of his research has many objectives, including:

Peter Haydock/The JASON Project

a. Identifying CO_2 point sources, such as power plants and refineries.
b. Evaluating potential geologic sequestration sites, or sinks.
c. Assessing the distance and transportation needed to move CO_2 from the sources to the potential sinks.

The overall goal of his research is to determine the most effective and safe technologies to capture and transport large amounts of carbon, that would otherwise be emitted into the atmosphere, from source to sink.

In this assignment, you will analyze Dr. Guthrie's data on carbon sources and potential sinks collected during Phase I of his research. Once you are done with the analysis, you will focus on your local region. You will identify the carbon sources that are within or nearest to your community. Then, you will assess the closest potential carbon sequestration sites or sinks, and determine the distance the CO_2 would need to be transported.

Materials
- **Mission 3 Field Assignment Data Sheet**
- **computer with Internet access**

Objectives:
- Analyze CO_2 point sources and population density throughout North America.
- Analyze maps of potential geologic sequestration sites (sinks) for carbon throughout North America.
- Research and explain the geologic events which lead to the development of these sequestration sites.
- Analyze CO_2 emissions and sources of your local area.
- Determine the storage size and locations of sequestration sinks in your state or nearby area.
- Calculate the rates at which the sequestration sinks could be filled.

Field Prep

1 Go to the NatCarb site online to obtain the latest CO_2 point sources map from NETL, or use the 2008 map in the data sheet to analyze carbon emissions across North America.

  a. What is the most common CO_2 source?

  b. Describe the distribution of CO_2 sources across the map. Which parts of the country contain higher and lower densities of CO_2 sources?

  c. Which states or parts of the country have higher densities of industrial sources, refineries/chemical sources, and ethanol plant sources of CO_2?

  d. Why do you think there is not an even distribution of the CO_2 sources across North America?

2 Compare and contrast the CO_2 sources map to the population density map in the data sheet. Does there appear to be any correlation between the two? If so, explain the correlation.

3 Analyze the potential geologic sequestration sink map in the data sheet. Determine which states or parts of the country have the easiest access to each of the following:

a. Oil and Natural Gas Fields: Oil and gas reservoirs already have many of the characteristics needed for geologic storage of CO_2. The geologic conditions at these locations already trap oil and gas which means they are favorable for CO_2 sequestration.

b. Unmineable Coal Seams: Coal has varying amounts of pore space within it that is normally filled with methane. These pore spaces could provide an excellent storage site for CO_2. By pumping the CO_2 into the coal, the methane can be pushed out and recovered to be used as fuel. The CO_2 will then take its place in the coal.

c. Deep Saline Formations: These layers of rocks are saturated with brine, or salty water. Since these reservoirs already trap and hold large amounts of liquid, they may provide enormous potential for CO_2 storage.

④ Based on the maps, which sink—oil and natural gas, coal, or deep saline—provides the largest area for potential carbon sequestration?

⑤ Research and explain the geologic events that lead to the development of the oil and natural gas, coal, and deep saline formations that are good sites for carbon sequestration. Share your research with your class.

Mission Challenge

❶ Analyze the summary chart of state or province CO_2 emissions.

a. Determine the levels of CO_2 emissions per year and number of sources for your state or province. Please note the level of CO_2 emissions from your state only includes the point sources, such as power plants and refineries, and does not include non-point sources, such as cars.

b. Determine the top three states or provinces based on CO_2 emissions per year.

❷ Use the interactive sources map on the NatCarb website to determine the location of the nearest point sources to your town. Use research tools to try and determine exactly what they are.

❸ Use the summary chart to determine the amount of potential storage for each source—oil and natural gas, coal, or deep saline—in your state and the top three carbon emitters. Include high and low estimates.

❹ Use the storage (sink) map and scale to determine the distance from your community or state to the closest sink in each category.

❺ Document the high and low estimates for total storage resources within your state and the top three emitters from the summary chart.

❻ Document the top three states, high and low estimates, for total storage resources from the summary chart.

Mission Debrief

❶ Calculate how many years it would take your state or province to fill the total storage resources within your state based on the low and high estimates of their size and if the CO_2 emissions of the point sources stay at the same rate.

a. Low estimate: Divide Total Storage Resource Low Estimate by CO_2 emissions for your state or province

b. High estimate: Divide Total Storage Resource High Estimate by CO_2 emissions for your state or province

❷ Calculate the time it would take to fill the total storage resources of all states and provinces based on the total CO_2 emissions of all point sources. Include low and high estimates.

Journal Question Dr. Guthrie and his team have focused their research on point sources of carbon, such as power plants and refineries, because the carbon from these facilities can be easily captured and stored. However, non-point sources, such as cars, also emit carbon into the atmosphere every year. Develop some ideas for how we could collect and store carbon from non-point sources and then effectively transport it to a sequestration sink.

CIVILIZATION UNDERCOVER

Otis Imboden/National Geographic Image Collection

Scientists today study natural disasters, such as earthquakes and volcanic eruptions, to help protect people who live in dangerous areas. But what about people who lived thousands of years ago, before there was any technology to monitor such hazards? Did they even know that they were living near volcanoes or along active fault lines? The story of Akrotiri provides us with some insight into this mystery.

Akrotiri was a bustling city on the Greek island of Santorini around 4,000 years ago. This was a prosperous city with large, multi-storied buildings and extensive drainage systems. Beautiful courtyards and magnificent wall paintings filled the homes and palaces of the residents of this island paradise. And then, in one short moment, the entire city was buried.

Archaeologists uncovered the city during excavations in 1967. In order to expose the city of Akrotiri, archaeologists had to dig through a thick layer of pumice, or volcanic rock. Scientists quickly realized that Akrotiri had been buried by a large eruption of the Santorini volcano.

The residents of Akrotiri probably understood that they were living on a volcano, but they probably did not know how dangerous it could be. The eruption that buried Akrotiri was one of the largest volcanic eruptions in history, sending plumes of ash and pumice 32 km (20 mi) into the sky! A layer of pumice over 60 meters (197 ft) thick covered the island of Santorini!

Lloyd K. Townsend/Wikimedia Commons

Otis Imboden/National Geographic Image Collection

Grodon Graham/National Geographic Image Collection

GREECE
AND THE AEGEAN

National Geographic Maps

What happened to the people of Akrotiri? Archaeologists believe that there was a large earthquake before the eruption, which warned the people that something was happening underneath the volcano. Even though they didn't have modern-day scientists to warn them that an eruption was imminent, archaeologists believe that most of the people living on Santorini were able to escape the catastrophic explosion.

Unfortunately, not everyone living near large volcanoes in ancient times was able to escape their deadly effects. The most famous example is Pompeii, Italy. During the eruption of Mount Vesuvius, ash fell from the sky for about twelve hours. Residents believed that they were safe from the more dangerous effects of the eruption, and remained in the city. However, a lethal pyroclastic flow, which is a fast moving current of hot gas and rock, reached the city and killed everyone.

Today, scientists understand how to avoid such tragedies and assist in the evacuation of people living near volcanoes. The Santorini volcano is still active today, and over one million visitors come to the island every year. Recently, Bob Ballard's team of geologists investigated the underwater part of the Santorini volcano—the caldera floor. Using remotely operated vehicles and sonar systems, the team searched for clues to learn more about the eruption. Bob and his team know that the more we understand about the eruptions of the past, the more prepared we will be for the eruptions in the future.

Otis Imboden/National Geographic Image Collection

Tino Soriano/National Geographic Image Collection

YOUR TURN

Research the geologic history of an active volcano using online or print resources. Then, draw a bird's eye view or topographic map of the volcano. Using Google Earth™, explore the surrounding area for evidence of past eruptions. Some things to look for are remnants of mass movement, fallen trees, ash, and layers of extrusive igneous rock. Draw this evidence on your map and create a legend to document your findings.

"By mapping the oceans, we can help predict how tsunamis will travel to places where people live, we can model the role oceans play in our climate system, we can manage and protect fish better, and we can learn how the world works."

—Dr. Walter Smith
Geophysicist, NOAA

Walter Smith

Walter Smith uses the radar altimeter on the Jason-2 and other satellites to study and map Earth's sea-floor geology. He is discovering, identifying, and analyzing the many features on the ocean floor that we never knew existed.

Meet the Researchers Video
Find out how Dr. Smith uses altimeter measurements from satellites that are orbiting Earth to study the bottom of the ocean.

Geophysicist, NOAA

Read more about Walter online in the JASON Mission Center.

Your Mission...

Journey through the oceans and Earth's outer layers to its core to better understand the dynamic nature of our planet.

To accomplish your mission successfully, you will need to

- Explore Earth's interior and ocean floor.
- Analyze the dynamic geologic processes that are moving continents on Earth's surface.
- Investigate models that explain the dynamic nature of Earth's lithosphere.
- Examine the relationships between plate tectonics, earthquakes, and volcanoes.
- Explore the instruments and methods used by scientists to monitor and provide safety recommendations for areas at risk from earthquakes and volcanic eruptions.

Join the Team

Dr. Walter Smith from NOAA shows Argonauts (L to R) Ben Brannan, Karina Jougla, Sachi Sanghavi, and Jodi Phipps how to compare the number and distribution of volcanoes found on land to what his satellite research is showing at the bottom of the ocean.

Peter Haydock/The JASON Project

Into the Deep

Standing on Mary's Peak, the tallest mountain in the Oregon Coastal Range at nearly 1,250 m (4,101 ft) tall, Dr. Walter Smith looks east to the mountains and volcanoes of the Cascade range and west to the Pacific Ocean. He understands that massive forces are at work here. By examining the rocks beneath his feet, he knows that where he stands was once at the bottom of the ocean. He also knows that just to the east in the Cascades, forces within Earth occasionally unleash their fury as massive eruptions. With 17 volcanoes in this chain, there have been over 50 eruptions in the past 4,000 years.

Look at a map of the world, and pay close attention to the oceans. You'll notice that all over the ocean floor, there are ridges that represent mountains and undersea landforms. But what about the spots that appear smooth? Does that mean that there isn't anything there? No! Actually, it just means that this part of the ocean has not been explored yet – and we don't know what features are there! As part of his exploration to discover what lies beneath the oceans, Walter uses satellites, like the Jason-2 satellite, to measure sea surface changes. Minute changes can reveal underwater volcanoes and mountains that help tell the story of our ever-changing Earth.

Walter has uncovered thousands of seamounts and many thousands of kilometers of new ridges and trenches. Each discovery helps to tell the story of plate tectonics. Each new feature holds the promise of much more. There may be a new and unique ecosystem waiting to be discovered or the supply to a new energy source or mineral resource that is in demand.

Mission 4 Briefing Video Prepare for your Mission by viewing this briefing on your objectives. Learn how Walter Smith discovers and analyzes the geologic features of the ocean floor which are produced by the forces from within Earth.

Mission Briefing

In This Section:

You Will Learn

What is the structure of Earth?

What have we learned from the ocean floor?

How do we think continents move?

This is Why

Exploring Earth's structure can provide insight as to how our planet works.

Stage 1: Structure of Earth

Exploring Change

Have you ever gone swimming in the ocean? If you have, did you ever wonder what was beneath you? There is an enormous unexplored world deep beneath the sea where much of the world's most exciting geologic events occur. The ocean floor accounts for more than 70 percent of Earth's entire surface. It is where the world's tallest mountains and deepest valleys are. The geologic processes below the ocean floor are generally more active than those on land, and have played a large part in forming many of the mountains, islands, and even continents of the world!

Dr. Walter Smith has dedicated his career to uncovering the mysteries of the deep seas so that we can better explain the changes we see and experience on land. These changes can be slow and gradual, like the formation of the majestic Himalayan Mountains, or quick and dynamic, like the two earthquakes that affected millions of lives in Haiti on January 12, 2010 and in Chile just a few weeks later on February 27, 2010. Regardless of how gradual or quick these changes are, many of their origins can be traced to processes occurring deep below the ocean floor.

Principle of Uniformitarianism

The study of geology can be called "the study of how Earth changes." Geologic changes over time have affected the distribution of rocks and minerals, the building up and breaking down of land formations, and the development of life that flourishes on Earth today.

The processes driving these changes have been happening for billions of years. This can be summarized by the **Principle of Uniformitarianism**, which states that geologic processes changing Earth's surface today worked the same way in the past. This has been the basis of much of what we know about our planet, since we can apply what we learn today to help understand what happened on Earth thousands, or millions, of years ago.

✔ **Check for Understanding**
What do we learn from the Principle of Uniformitarianism?

Continental Drift

In the late 1500s, Flemish cartographer Abraham Ortelius noted that the continents on his map looked as though they fit together like a puzzle. He deduced that the continents may have been connected at one time, and had somehow moved. Observations such as this led to the initial concept of **continental drift**, a theory that the continents were once connected and have been slowly moving over time.

Pangaea

Alfred Wegener, a German meteorologist, scientist, and polar researcher, expanded on the theory of continental drift in 1912 by pointing out the similarities between rocks, geologic structures, and fossils across the Atlantic Ocean. He also noted that the shape of the coastline on the western side of Africa matched South America's eastern coastline.

Based on his observations, Wegener proposed that a supercontinent composed of all of the current continents once existed. He called this supercontinent **Pangaea**, Greek for "all lands." He argued that forces within Earth broke Pangaea into two continents, **Laurasia** and **Gondwanaland**. Over time, these two land masses divided even further into the continents we see today.

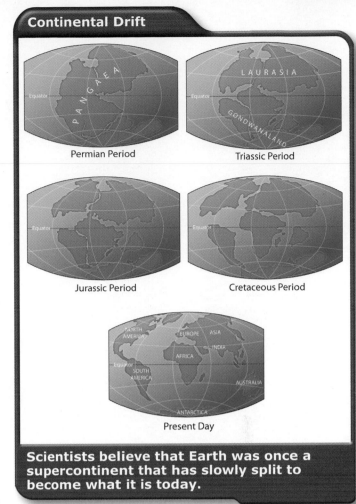

Continental Drift

Permian Period

Triassic Period

Jurassic Period

Cretaceous Period

Present Day

Scientists believe that Earth was once a supercontinent that has slowly split to become what it is today.

Despite evidence supporting continental drift, the idea of massive continents moving created heated debates. How did these land masses move apart?

Convection

In the early 1930s, British geologist Arthur Holmes thought about mechanisms inside Earth that could move continents on the surface. Holmes speculated that deep below the surface was a layer of molten rock. This molten rock was heated by the center of the planet. Through the process of **convection**, this heated rock would rise toward the surface. Near the surface it would cool and sink back down, producing convection currents. Holmes proposed that these convection currents were strong enough to move entire continents!

Unfortunately, the technology at the time limited Holmes' ability to investigate his theory. To investigate further, scientists needed to develop a way to look deep into Earth.

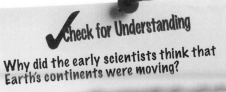
✔ **Check for Understanding**
Why did the early scientists think that Earth's continents were moving?

Picture Earth as a giant apple with its center located more than 6,000 km (3,728 mi) deep. You would be hard pressed to know what is actually inside that apple if you could hardly make it past the peel! So how do we know what is inside Earth when we have barely even scratched the surface?

Technology has allowed us to probe deep into our planet using wave monitoring devices. In fact, the very things that cause some of the destruction and devastation we see around the world—seismic or earthquake waves—are used to help better understand the structure of the planet. When seismic waves encounter material of different composition, the direction in which they travel is altered. By monitoring the path of seismic waves, scientists have been able to map out the different layers deep below the surface.

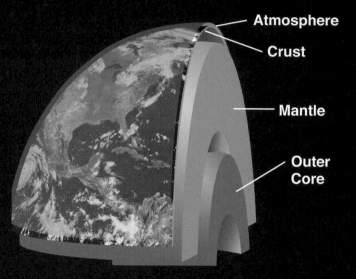

Atmosphere

Crust

Mantle

Outer Core

Earth's Outermost Layer

Earth's outermost layer is commonly known as the **crust**. We are most familiar with this part of the planet because we live on it. Like the hard shell of an egg, it is very thin and brittle compared to what lies deep beneath it. Earth's crust is thinnest along the ocean floor, averaging about 7 km (4.3 mi) in thickness. This part of the crust is called oceanic crust and is composed of dense **mafic** rocks, such as basalt and gabbro.

The part of Earth we live on is called the continental crust. It is generally thicker (30-100 km or 19-62 mi) and made of less dense **felsic** rock, such as granite. The density difference between oceanic and continental crust affects the way they interact during collisions.

Deeper into Earth

Venturing deeper into Earth, we find the thickest section of the planet (2,900 km or 1,802 mi) called the **mantle**. The uppermost portion of the mantle is much different than the regions beneath it. It is about 100 km (62 mi) thick, and is hard like the crust. Combined with Earth's crust, this area is called the **lithosphere**. The rigid nature of the lithosphere causes it to break up into giant slabs of rock called **lithospheric** or **tectonic plates**. These plates float and move on top of the **asthenosphere**, the part of the mantle just below the lithosphere. The combination of temperature and pressure makes the asthenosphere gooey and ductile. Scientists describe this part of the mantle as being "weak" because it is able to compress, stretch, and flow like Silly Putty®.

As we go deeper into the mantle, temperature and pressure increases. The effect of temperature softens rocks, while the effect of pressure makes them stronger. These two contradictory tendencies interact in a complex way to form the "stronger" **mesosphere**, the lower portion of the mantle.

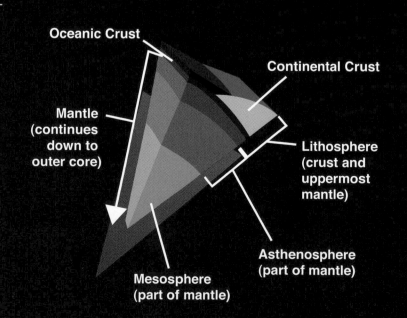

Oceanic Crust

Continental Crust

Mantle (continues down to outer core)

Lithosphere (crust and uppermost mantle)

Asthenosphere (part of mantle)

Mesosphere (part of mantle)

Earth's Core

Seismic waves have also helped us probe deep into Earth's **core**. We have learned that the core of our planet is divided into two parts, the liquid outer core and the solid inner core. Together they represent about 15 percent of Earth's volume, and have a diameter of about 3,480 km (2,162 mi).

The intense heat from the solid inner core and the rotation of Earth causes the liquid outer core to move in convection currents. This moving liquid is thought to cause the magnetic field that surrounds Earth.

It is theorized that both parts of the core are composed mainly of iron. Some scientists have even speculated that the solid inner core is a giant iron crystal that is slightly smaller than the moon! The inner core is around 4,500°C (8,132°F). The liquid outer core is around 3,550°C (6,422°F), which is about three to four times hotter than the lava that erupts from volcanoes.

Outer Core of Molten Metal

Inner Core of Solid Metal

NASA

✓Check for Understanding

If you could slice Earth in half, what might you see?

Why can Earth's crust be described as cracked?

Journey to the Sea Floor

Due to low temperatures, lack of light, and pressure, the majority of the ocean floor is inhospitable to humans. However, technological advances have enabled scientists to map areas of the ocean floor. This technology is based on the same principal used by bats and beluga whales for getting around—sound waves and echoes. Sonar monitors and measures echoes to determine the distance to an object. Interest in sonar technology was largely influenced by war efforts during the early 20th century. The need to detect enemy submarines advanced sonar to a point where remarkable sea-floor topography was discovered.

Mid-Ocean Ridge

Before the invention of sonar, very little was known about the ocean floor. Early line sounding devices, which were weights attached to spools of rope, uncovered some elevation differences that lead people to believe the ocean floor had a varied topography. The development of sonar technology in the early 20th century confirmed this and uncovered more mountains along the sea floor. The discovery of the **mid-ocean ridge**, a mountain range at the bottom of the ocean, sparked great interest in the field of oceanography because it generated many questions. How does a feature of this size form on the ocean floor? What geologic processes are happening?

Today, Dr. Walter Smith's maps of the ocean floor show us that the mid-ocean ridge curves through all the oceans of the world like the seams of a baseball. Running down the middle of this mountain range is a valley called a **rift**.

Explorer's Connection

During the early days of deep sea exploration, Dr. Bob Ballard's commute to work was not conventional by any means. He didn't have to worry about traffic jams or being late for meetings. He had to deal with the extreme dangers associated with navigating in total darkness, the excessive pressure caused by the ocean's weight, and a limited supply of oxygen!

Commuting in a submarine to the ocean floor took about two and a half hours. Limited by the oxygen in the tanks, he was able to work about three hours, saving just enough oxygen for the two and a half hour trip back to the surface.

That's five hours of commuting time for just three hours of work, and traveling an average distance of  less than 2 km (1.2 mi)! Understanding that there is more than 67,000 km (41,632 mi) of mid-ocean ridge to explore, Dr. Bob Ballard has introduced unmanned underwater robotic systems that help make deep sea ocean explorations much more efficient.

The curved green region running through the major oceans of the world is the mid-ocean ridge.

Sea-floor Spreading

American geologist Harry Hess was very interested in mid-ocean ridges. He thought that by understanding how the mid-ocean ridge formed, he could finally discover the mechanism behind continental drift.

In 1960, Hess proposed the idea of **sea-floor spreading**. He hypothesized that the rift that runs like a spine down the middle of the mid-ocean ridge is a continuous series of **vents**, or cracks in Earth's crust. These openings enable lava to erupt from the mantle. As hot lava erupts into the cool sea water, it instantly cools and hardens, becoming new oceanic crust. Over time, successive eruptions push older solidified rock outwards, gradually spreading apart the mid-ocean ridge and moving continents. This was a remarkable theory, but at the time, nobody was able to find proof that lava was erupting from the rift of the mid-ocean ridge.

Finding the Proof

During more than 120 underwater expeditions, Dr. Bob Ballard has explored the changes happening on Earth that have been occurring for millions of years. In 1977, while investigating a small section of the mid-ocean ridge near the Galápagos Islands of Ecuador, he discovered a key piece of evidence to explain how and why the continents moved.

Fast Fact

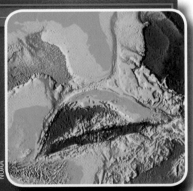

On April 6, 2010, British scientists discovered the deepest known hydrothermal vents, or black smokers, about 5 km (3.1 mi) below the Caribbean Sea in the Cayman Trench. Surrounding the black smokers, a dense concentration of life thrives off the chemicals and heat ejecting from the massive chimneys. This discovery has provided scientists with an opportunity to study the deep sea communities and the geology of valuable minerals deposited near these formations. As remote sensing technology continues to improve, so will our knowledge of the deep oceans.

Team Highlight

Walter Smith models how features at the bottom of the ocean form through crustal movements of Earth's ocean plates. All throughout the ocean, mountains form at sea floor spreading zones.

Venturing 2.7 km (1.7 mi) deep into the ocean and engulfed in total darkness, Dr. Ballard was searching for volcanic heat that could explain the formation of mid-ocean ridges. His team discovered what looked like the giant pipes of a church organ. These pipe-like structures, hydrothermal vents, continuously spewed darks clouds of minerals reaching temperatures of 350°C (662°F)! The high temperatures indicated that the rift was where the sea floor was literally being ripped apart and molten rock erupting through the surface to was forming new earth. Bob Ballard's discovery has helped shape our current understanding of how continents move, why earthquakes occur, and where and when volcanoes erupt.

✓ Check for Understanding

Why was Dr. Ballard exploring the mid-ocean ridge?

Theory of Plate Tectonics

After Alfred Wegener presented his idea of continental drift, scientists began collecting more evidence which supported the concept that Earth's crust was indeed moving. By the 1960s, many scientists were beginning to agree upon the theory of **plate tectonics**. This theory states that the lithosphere is broken into multiple rigid tectonic plates, similar to a cracked shell of a hard-boiled egg. These tectonic plates are slowly being moved in different directions by convection currents in the hot mantle.

Plate Boundaries

Different tectonic plates interact with one another at the plate boundaries. Tectonic plates are not all moving in the same direction. Plates moving into each other form **convergent boundaries**, plates moving apart from each other form **divergent boundaries**, and plates sliding next to each other form **transform boundaries**. These boundaries are significant because they are where changes, such as earthquakes and volcanic activity, generally occur.

Today, the theory of plate tectonics is almost universally accepted by scientists. It helps explain a vast number of geologic phenomena that could not be explained in the past. Armed with an understanding of the basic mechanisms that shape our planet, geologists—and you—are now able to better understand how many of the landforms on Earth have been formed, from the Himalayas to the Grand Canyon, and from the mid-ocean ridge to the Mariana Trench.

✓Check for Understanding

Describe the three types of plate boundaries.

Mapping the Ocean Floor

Discoveries along the ocean floor have provided evidence of large scale geologic changes, like continental drift, and supported theories, like plate tectonics. Scientists believe that the ocean floor can tell us much more about the geologic processes on Earth. However, humans generally cannot see below 50 m (164 ft) from the surface because most of the entire ocean area is covered in eternal darkness. The water that covers the ocean floor has proven to be such an obstacle that even today, we know more about the surface features of the moon, Venus, and Mars than many parts of our own oceans!

As a result, Dr. Walter Smith must rely on state-of-the-art technology to map the ocean floor. He analyzes streams of data from orbiting satellites that detect slight changes in elevation on the ocean's surface.

Why does the elevation change matter? **Gravity** is the force of attraction between two objects, and is directly proportional to an object's mass. Therefore, the larger the object's mass, the larger its gravitational field. The gravitational field of a massive underwater volcano, called a **seamount,** will attract more water molecules to it than a smaller seamount. This results in the appearance of a slight bulge on the ocean's surface just above the seamount that can be detected by satellites. By scouring the ocean surface for these bulges, Walter is able to generate maps of the ocean floor.

The maps that Dr. Smith produces are helping us solve many mysteries of our planet. His maps provide areas of safe passage for boats and submarines, a better understanding of the geologic processes that continue to shape our planet, and information to improve weather forecasts that are affected by ocean currents.

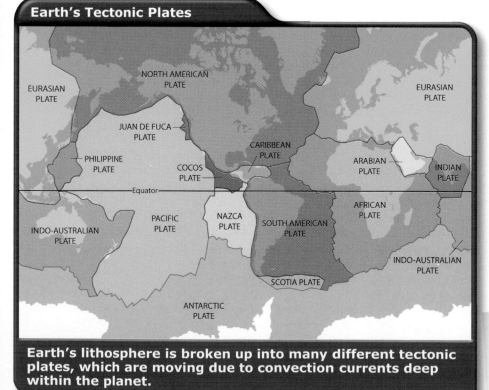

Earth's Tectonic Plates

EURASIAN PLATE

NORTH AMERICAN PLATE

EURASIAN PLATE

JUAN DE FUCA PLATE

PHILIPPINE PLATE

CARIBBEAN PLATE

ARABIAN PLATE

INDIAN PLATE

COCOS PLATE

Equator

PACIFIC PLATE

NAZCA PLATE

SOUTH AMERICAN PLATE

AFRICAN PLATE

INDO-AUSTRALIAN PLATE

INDO-AUSTRALIAN PLATE

SCOTIA PLATE

ANTARCTIC PLATE

Earth's lithosphere is broken up into many different tectonic plates, which are moving due to convection currents deep within the planet.

✓Check for Understanding

What are some challenges to mapping the ocean floor?

The Moving Surface

Even though more than 70 percent of Earth's surface is covered in water and a majority of this area has never been explored, Walter Smith is continually updating his maps of the ocean floor. Using the data provided by satellites, he has discovered a range of landforms that exist on the ocean floor, including ocean trenches, mountains, and underwater volcanoes. Many of these features are believed to be associated with tectonic plate movement. As a result, his maps provide scientists with the ability to see things they never knew existed before, and help them develop better models of the tectonic processes that are shaping Earth's surface.

In this activity, you will model a theory of convection that may be causing the tectonic plates to move and creating the features Dr. Smith sees on his maps. Using this model, you will then experiment with factors that may affect the convection process and the features created at the surface.

Materials

- **Lab 1 Data Sheet**
- **clear baking dish**
- **vegetable oil**
- **container of dried spices**
- **spoon**
- **polystyrene pieces**
- **supports for baking dish**
- **string**
- **ruler**
- **tape**
- **heat source**
- **marker**

Lab Prep

1. Place the clear baking dish on the supports in the center of the table.

2. Fill the dish at least half full with oil and mix a spoonful of spice into the oil.

3. Use the ruler, tape, and string to divide the dish into four equal quadrants: A, B, C, and D.

4. Place the heat source under the middle of the dish as shown in the data sheet.

5. Heat for about five minutes, then make observations.

Make Observations

1. Describe the effect of the heat source on the oil in different parts of the dish by observing the movement of the spice (e.g., near the edges, on top of the oil and near the bottom of the oil).

2. Predict what you think will happen if you put a piece of polystyrene in each quadrant.

3. Test your hypothesis by placing the polystyrene in quadrant A. Record your results. Continue for each quadrant. How did your predictions compare with your observations?

4. How could you make two pieces pull away from each other? Try it and record your observations. What does this represent?

5. How could you make one piece crash into the other? Try it and record your observations. What does this represent?

6. Coat the top of the oil with spice. Looking from the side, observe and describe the movement of spice in the oil. Observe and describe the interaction between the spice in the oil and the spice on top.

7. What part of Earth does the spice layer on top represent? What part of Earth does the oil represent? What part of Earth does the heat source represent? What type of plate boundary was created in the spice layer?

8. Look at the plate boundary and topographic maps in the data sheet. Find and highlight the boundaries where the type of crustal movement you observed in your dish is occurring.

9. Describe some features that are created at or near these locations.

Extension

Design an experiment using a different variable, such as adding heat sources or changing the heat source location, temperature, or thickness of lithosphere. With your instructor's approval, conduct your experiment.

 Journal Question Describe the processes which may cause Earth's lithosphere to move and break at the surface.

In This Section:
You Will Learn

What is an earthquake?

What causes earthquakes?

What are the consequences of earthquakes?

This is Why

Learning about earthquakes can help us develop strategies to protect people and property.

Stage 2: Earthquakes
What is an Earthquake?

Earthquakes are the sudden movements of Earth's crust that usually occur at plate boundaries. You may have never experienced an earthquake, but you probably have heard about the devastation caused by the large one that struck Port-au-Prince, Haiti on January 12, 2010. The first of many earthquakes to strike this region struck just before 5 p.m., and toppled buildings and homes, caused casualties, and affected more than a million lives!

Earthquakes happen every day around the world. Many release a small amount of energy only detectable by specialized instruments. Other earthquakes, like the one that struck Haiti, can be so devastating that there is a call to action for the world to unite, reach out, contribute to disaster relief efforts, and help rebuild a nation.

Living in **seismic zones**, areas where earthquake activity occurs frequently and consistently, can be dangerous. Geologists and engineers are working hard to understand how earthquakes work and are using this information to construct buildings that can withstand these types of natural disasters.

Folds and Faults

Today, scientists agree that Earth's rigid lithosphere is broken up into giant slabs of moving rock, commonly known as tectonic plates. This has been confirmed by precise measurements using signals from orbiting satellites that have monitored movement and detected even the smallest millimeters of change.

Plates can crash into, slip under, slide over, and rub next to other plates at plate boundaries. However, plates can sometimes get stuck due to the friction between them. When this happens, stress gradually builds up as convection currents in the mantle continue to move the tectonic plates.

When the stress can no longer be tolerated by the rock, the plates will move. The force generated by the moving plates causes rocks at the surface to fold and sometimes break. **Folds** occur when rock layers are squeezed together and double up or bend over other rock layers. **Faults** are breaks in Earth's crust caused by movement of one side of the break relative to the other. The type of fault that forms is determined by the direction the plates move. In **normal faults**, Earth's surface moves downwards relative to the fault. In **reverse faults**, Earth's surface moves upwards relative to the fault. **Strike-slip faults** form as the plates move horizontally past one another with very little vertical movement.

▲ The remnants of a collapsed overpass in San Fernando Valley, California are a reminder of the destruction earthquakes can cause.

Sudden plate movements, like slipping or sliding near fault planes, can release stored energy and cause earthquakes. Through geologic time, the forces that result from moving tectonic plates have caused some extremely destructive earthquakes, as well as some of the world's most spectacular land features.

✓ Check for Understanding

How do faults and folds form?

Tectonic Plate Boundaries

The majority of earthquakes around the world occur at tectonic plate boundaries. At these locations, rocks experience a great deal of stress caused by the force generated by moving tectonic plates. The types of forces, land features, and resulting earthquakes are determined by how tectonic plates interact at these boundaries.

Convergent Boundary

Occurs when two tectonic plates move into one another. When two plates of equal density converge, they can buckle and push upwards or sideways. If the converging plates are unequal in density, the more dense plate can be **subducted**, or pulled beneath the plate of lower density.

Type of Force
- **Compression forces** slowly squeeze rocks, until they either fold or break.

Features and Faults
- Synclines and anticlines can form if compression forces cause rocks to fold.
- When rocks break under compression, the rock moves upwards relative to the fault and forms a reverse fault.
- **Trenches** can form when dense oceanic crust subducts beneath less dense continental or oceanic crust.
- Mountains can form as plates buckle and are pushed upward.

Divergent Boundary

Occurs when two tectonic plates move away from one another. Much of Earth's new crust that forms deep along the ocean floor is caused by tectonic plate divergence. Dr. Walter Smith's sea-floor mapping work is shedding light upon deep sea divergent boundaries, and is helping us locate and better understand the landforms, earthquakes, and tsunamis that result from these tectonic plate interactions.

Type of Force
- As plates move apart, **tension forces** stretch and thin rocks in the middle.

Features and Faults
- When rocks break under tension, the rock moves downward relative to the fault and forms a normal fault.
- Rifts, like the Great Rift Valley in East Africa and the mid-ocean ridge, form as the plates move apart.

Transform Boundary

Occurs when tectonic plates slide horizontally past one another. Earthquakes occur at these boundaries as giant slabs of rock can often get stuck, and then suddenly slip past one another.

Type of Force
- **Shear forces** result as plates slide past other plates, and can cause rocks to break, change shape, or even slip apart.

Features and Faults
- When rocks break under shear forces, opposite sides of the break will slide horizontally past each other with very little vertical movement, forming a strike-slip fault.

Tectonic Plate Boundary Photo Gallery
View examples of the landforms that exist at tectonic plate boundaries.

NASA

Elements of an Earthquake

There is a lot of energy associated with earthquakes. The energy released by the moving plates is carried throughout the planet by **seismic waves**. The types of seismic waves earthquakes generate include primary, secondary, and surface waves.

Special instruments are placed all over Earth's surface to detect seismic waves and to monitor their size and speed. Using this information, scientists can learn many things about earthquakes.

Primary Waves

Primary waves, or P waves, are the fastest waves generated by an earthquake. These are usually the first waves to reach Earth's surface, hence their name. They can travel through both solid rock and liquids.

Primary waves are **compression waves** and move by squeezing and stretching the rock they travel through. The squeezing and stretching motion occurs in the same direction as the wave travels. An observer feeling the effects of a P wave might describe the ground as vibrating back and forth.

Secondary Waves

Secondary waves, or S waves, arrive after P waves because they are slower. They are **transverse waves**, transferring the energy of an earthquake by vibrating the ground up and down and sideways. S waves usually cause buildings to shake. Unlike P waves, S waves cannot move through liquid. It is this property of S waves that helped scientists determine that Earth's outer core is liquid.

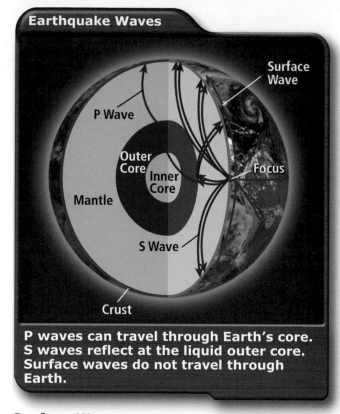

Earthquake Waves

P waves can travel through Earth's core. S waves reflect at the liquid outer core. Surface waves do not travel through Earth.

Surface Waves

Other types of waves that transfer the energy released by earthquakes are **surface waves**. Of the waves produced by earthquakes, these move the slowest, but are responsible for most of the damage associated with earthquakes—especially ones that originate near the surface. There are two types of surface waves. **Love waves** move the ground from side-to-side, and **Rayleigh waves** cause the ground to move like waves rolling through the ocean.

Focus and Epicenter

The location of where an earthquake originates is its **focus**. The focus is usually beneath Earth's surface. Seismic waves need to travel some distance before reaching the surface. The time it takes for people to feel the earthquake depends largely upon the distance from the focus. The potential for damage caused by an earthquake greatly increases if the focus is close to the surface. The **epicenter** is the location on Earth's surface that is directly above the focus of an earthquake.

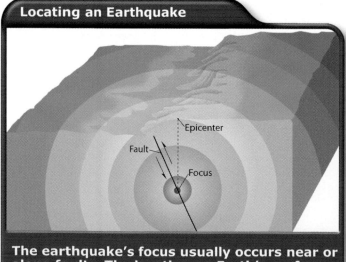

Locating an Earthquake

The earthquake's focus usually occurs near or along faults. The location on Earth's surface directly above the focus is the epicenter.

✓ **Check for Understanding**

Compare the different types of waves that can be produced by an earthquake.

Studying Earthquakes

So far, earthquakes have been described as small enough to go unnoticed or large enough to cause damage. However, there are more technical ways to describe an earthquake's size and impact on society. **Seismology** is the study of earthquakes, and seismologists are scientists who study earthquakes. They use specialized instruments to help them predict, record, monitor, and measure earthquakes.

Seismographs

Seismologists use specialized instruments called **seismographs** to detect waves that transfer an earthquake's energy. Some are so sensitive that they can detect even the smallest vibrations in Earth's crust caused by waves, or even traffic.

Today, most seismographs are computerized. They collect data from earthquakes and almost instantly analyze this data. Early seismographs worked by graphing the P, S, and surface waves generated by an earthquake on paper using a pen and a weight suspended from a frame. These drawings were called seismograms. Large earthquakes would move the pen more dramatically, creating a seismogram with a large amplitude. Smaller earthquakes would not move the pen much and would create seismograms with a smaller amplitude.

The different speeds at which surface waves travel make it possible for seismologists to calculate the distance between the location of the seismograph and epicenter of the earthquake.

The epicenter can be established using the time interval between the initial P wave and the S wave from seismograph readings. Charts correlating P and S wave time intervals with epicenter distances can be used to determine the distance the seismograph is from the epicenter.

Seismographs are placed all over the world to continually record and monitor earthquake activity on the entire planet. Data collected from these stations help scientists monitor changes in Earth's crust so that they can better predict the occurrence and magnitude of the next major earthquake.

Waves carry the energy released by an earthquake outwards in all directions. Seismographs placed on Earth's surface will detect the quicker P waves first, while the detection of slower moving S waves and surface waves will follow. Because only P and S waves are able to travel below the surface of Earth, they are used to determine the focus of an earthquake using triangulation.

What is Triangulation?

A single seismograph can only establish the distance it is away from the epicenter of an earthquake. Seismologists identify the epicenter of an earthquake by using the epicenter distances of three different seismographs, known as triangulation.

The radius of each circle represents the distance the seismograph is away from the epicenter. The intersection point of the circles is the approximate location of the epicenter.

Earthquake Epicenter

Earthquake Magnitude

You may have heard news reports referring to earthquake magnitude readings, such as the magnitude 7 earthquake in Haiti, the magnitude 8.8 earthquake in Chile, and the magnitude 7.2 earthquake in Baja California, Mexico, in 2010. **Magnitude** is the measure of an earthquake's relative size. There are several ways that seismologists can measure magnitude, based upon the type of seismograph used and seismic wave measured. Some measures of magnitude are based upon P and S waves that travel within Earth, while others are based on Love and Rayleigh waves that travel along or near Earth's surface.

The original earthquake magnitude scale was developed in 1935 by Dr. Charles Richter. The **Richter scale** combined mathematics with seismograph data so that scientists could compare earthquakes around the world. Due to technological advances, the Richter scale has been replaced by the **moment-magnitude scale** we use today. Both are scales based on a logarithm of the wave amplitude recorded by seismographs. This means that, while the shaking of a magnitude 7 earthquake is 10 times greater than a magnitude 6 earthquake, the energy released by a magnitude 7 earthquake is approximately 32 times greater than the magnitude 6 earthquake.

Earthquakes that make news reports are usually greater than magnitude 4.5, because tremors below magnitude 4.5 can go unnoticed by many people. There are several thousand of these earthquakes recorded each year! Earthquakes above magnitude 4.5 garner more attention because of the damage they can cause. Scientists hypothesize that earthquakes surpassing magnitudes of 9 are very rare, because the lithosphere is rigid and does not usually have the capacity to store the energy necessary to produce such a large earthquake. This is reassuring news as events like the December 26, 2004 magnitude 9.1 earthquake, and the tsunami it caused near the island of Sumatra, illustrate how devastating they can be.

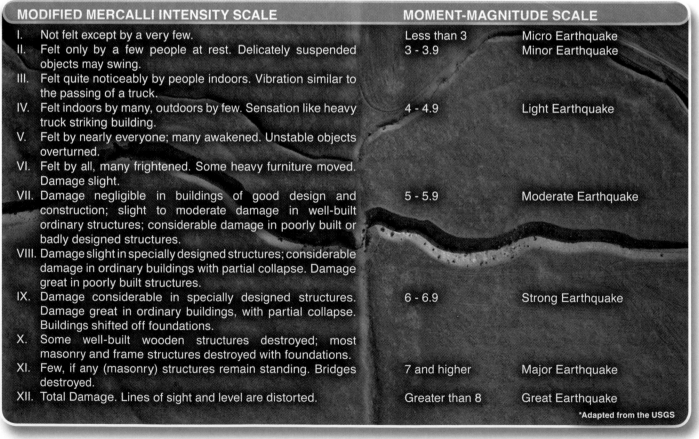

MODIFIED MERCALLI INTENSITY SCALE	MOMENT-MAGNITUDE SCALE	
I. Not felt except by a very few.	Less than 3	Micro Earthquake
II. Felt only by a few people at rest. Delicately suspended objects may swing.	3 - 3.9	Minor Earthquake
III. Felt quite noticeably by people indoors. Vibration similar to the passing of a truck.		
IV. Felt indoors by many, outdoors by few. Sensation like heavy truck striking building.	4 - 4.9	Light Earthquake
V. Felt by nearly everyone; many awakened. Unstable objects overturned.		
VI. Felt by all, many frightened. Some heavy furniture moved. Damage slight.		
VII. Damage negligible in buildings of good design and construction; slight to moderate damage in well-built ordinary structures; considerable damage in poorly built or badly designed structures.	5 - 5.9	Moderate Earthquake
VIII. Damage slight in specially designed structures; considerable damage in ordinary buildings with partial collapse. Damage great in poorly built structures.		
IX. Damage considerable in specially designed structures. Damage great in ordinary buildings, with partial collapse. Buildings shifted off foundations.	6 - 6.9	Strong Earthquake
X. Some well-built wooden structures destroyed; most masonry and frame structures destroyed with foundations.		
XI. Few, if any (masonry) structures remain standing. Bridges destroyed.	7 and higher	Major Earthquake
XII. Total Damage. Lines of sight and level are distorted.	Greater than 8	Great Earthquake

*Adapted from the USGS

James P. Blair/National Geographic Image Collection

The Modified Mercalli Intensity Scale

The magnitude of an earthquake doesn't always translate to how much damage it causes. Sometimes, an earthquake with a lower magnitude can cause even more damage than one with a greater magnitude.

The **Modified Mercalli Intensity scale** measures the effect that an earthquake has on populated areas. This scale is based upon observation and reports of shaking and damage done to structures. Therefore, it is only applicable to locations where there are people. Earthquakes in remote locations or in the ocean cannot be measured using this scale.

It is designated using 12 increasing levels of intensity represented by the Roman numerals I – XII. A location where people do not feel any ground movement would have an intensity of I. At an intensity of VI, everyone would feel the ground move, and there would be some damage. An area where almost everything is destroyed would have an intensity reading of XII.

✔check for Understanding

Compare the moment-magnitude scale and the Modified Mercalli Intensity scale.

Consequences of Earthquakes

News images of earthquakes often show damaged buildings, burst water mains, fires, and human casualties. Destruction like this is usually from strong earthquakes with epicenters close to major cities. Earthquakes affect not only the human-made structures, but they can also affect soil and water through tsunamis, mass movement, and liquefaction.

▼ The magnitude 8.8 earthquake that occurred in Chile on February 27, 2010 shifted the city of Concepción about three meters (9.8 ft) west!

Fast Fact

A part of Dr. Walter Smith's sea floor mapping work is to locate and map seamounts. It is estimated that there are over 100,000 more seamounts still undiscovered.

On January 8, 2005, the U.S.S. San Francisco submarine collided with an unmapped seamount near the Caroline Islands at a depth of about 160 m (525 ft). The entire bow was shattered, killing one sailor and injuring 23 more. Since that accident, Dr. Smith's work has been used by the U.S. Navy so that future accidents can be avoided.

Tsunamis

Earthquakes that occur below the ocean floor can sometimes trigger a massive water wave called a **tsunami**. These waves are created when tremendous amounts of energy released by an earthquake move the sea floor. This movement can be caused by shifting plates on the sea floor or even underwater landslides. The energy from this sudden movement can be transferred to the surrounding water, forming a potentially devastating tsunami wave.

On December 26, 2004, a tsunami in the Indian Ocean Basin took more than 200,000 lives. This tsunami was caused by a massive magnitude 9.1 undersea earthquake off the west coast of Northern Sumatra, Indonesia.

Mass Movement

Mass movement triggered by earthquakes, like landslides, rock falls, and mudflows, can also cause major damage. Seismic waves can shake and loosen soil and rock. If this material is located on a slope, large amounts of material can tumble downhill. The tumbling material can move as one giant mass, or it can break up into smaller pieces as a deadly river of soil and rock. Depending on the amount of moving material, landslides have the potential to engulf and destroy any object in their path.

Liquefaction

Is the area in which you live built on solid rock, gravel, sand, or a mixture of these? If you live in an area built on top of loose material, like sand, liquefaction can further increase the damage caused by an earthquake, especially if water is nearby. **Liquefaction** is the phenomenon that occurs when the shaking motion of an earthquake causes water-saturated sediment to temporarily lose strength and act as if it were a liquid. Three factors required for liquefaction to occur are: loose sand and silt grains, water filling the spaces between sand and silt grains, and strong shaking. The soil that undergoes liquefaction loses the ability to support structures, like buildings and homes. This may lead to the tilting or toppling of buildings, as well as damage to underground utilities, like gas and sewage pipes.

USGS

▲ The magnitude 7.5 earthquake that struck Niigata, Japan, in June 1964 caused the land to undergo liquefaction, resulting in major damage to buildings and homes.

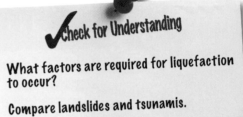

✓ Check for Understanding

What factors are required for liquefaction to occur?

Compare landslides and tsunamis.

Earthquake Protection Strategies

❶ Fasten pictures, bookcases, and tall dressers to walls. Avoid placing large objects that can fall near your bed. Place heavier objects at the bottom of shelves to increase stability, and store breakable objects and any flammable or corrosive liquids on shelves with latches.

❷ Designate a safe place where you can remain until the earthquake stops. If you are indoors during an earthquake, seek shelter under a sturdy desk or table, and stay clear of areas where glass or heavy bookcases can fall. If you are outdoors during an earthquake, stay away from buildings, trees, telephone cables, and electrical lines.

❸ Make an earthquake emergency kit. Include enough non-perishable food and water for three days, and pack a first-aid kit with sterile bandages, soap, latex gloves, sunscreen, gauze pads, tweezers, antiseptic, scissors, and a thermometer. Also have extra batteries, a flashlight and a battery operated radio.

❹ Develop a plan in case family members are separated from one another. Designate a common area where family members can meet. Designate a contact person and make sure everyone knows their phone number.

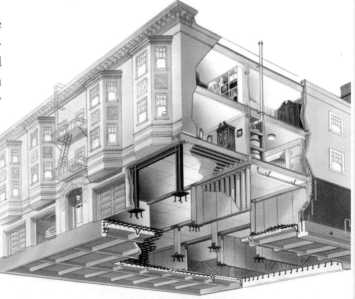

Richard Leech/National Geographic Image Collection

Modeling Earthquakes

Earthquakes are some of most devastating geologic events that affect people and property. We know that earthquakes are associated with plate boundaries, but a majority of these boundaries are covered by the world's oceans. This means that our understanding of what is happening in these areas is much less than the areas we can observe on land. Using the data from his satellites, Walter Smith is creating maps of the ocean floor which are helping us understand these underwater areas where earthquakes occur, and focus on what effect these events have on the land and on the buildings we construct.

In this activity, you will analyze the effect of sediment type on how the ground reacts to a simulated earthquake, and investigate the effect of the sediment and earthquake on model structures.

Materials

- Lab 2 Data Sheet
- 2 containers of the same size
- 2 types of sediment (e.g., sand, soil)
- masking tape
- marker
- 5 craft sticks
- 4 rocks
- water
- large spoon
- stop watch
- graduated cylinder

Lab Prep

1. Prepare the containers of saturated sediment by following the setup procedures in the data sheet.

Make Observations

1. Using the palm of your hand or a rubber mallet, firmly tap the side of container A in a rhythmic way to create vibrations for 30 seconds. This models the earthquake.

2. Observe, measure, and document the effect of the earthquake vibrations on different areas of the sediment, water in the sediment, craft sticks, and rocks.

3. Remove the craft sticks and rocks. Mix the sand and water thoroughly so there is no standing water at the surface.

4. Place the craft sticks at the same grid locations and push each one 2 cm into the sediment.

5. Place the rocks at the same location as the first trial. Repeat steps 1 and 2.

6. Describe the similarities and differences between trial 1 and 2.

7. Repeat steps 1 to 6 using container B, placing the sticks and rocks in the same locations as container A.

8. Compare and contrast the effects of the earthquake on the two types of sediment.

9. If the craft sticks and rocks represent buildings and human-made structures, what are some areas of concern to consider in earthquake-prone regions?

10. Develop some strategies for stabilizing the buildings, and conduct an experiment analyzing the effect of your strategies. Report your results to the class.

11. Compare and contrast the seismic hazard-liquefaction map with the geologic map of San Francisco in the data sheet.

    a. What types of surface cover are most and least prone to liquefaction in this area?

    b. What types of surface cover are most and least prone to earthquake-induced landslides in this area?

    c. Develop some hypotheses about why these types of surface cover are most and least prone to liquefaction or earthquake-induced landslides.

Extension

Experiment with other sediment types and share your results with your class.

 Journal Question Based on what you have learned, describe some major cities which may experience liquefaction, and provide your reasoning.

This is Why

Understanding volcanoes can help society weigh the advantages and limitations of living in regions of volcanic activity.

Stage 3: Volcanoes
What is a Volcano?

When you picture a volcano, you probably think of a massive cone-shaped mountain spewing lava, volcanic ash, and gas. While some volcanoes look like this, not all do. Volcanoes are not always cone-shaped and they are not always above ground. In fact, scientists estimate that approximately 80 percent of Earth's volcanoes are located underwater!

A **volcano** is any opening in Earth's crust where hot molten rock, ashes, gases, and rock fragments erupt. By transporting material that was once inside Earth to the surface, volcanoes are the primary way that Earth builds land.

Eruptions

An **eruption** occurs whenever molten rock, debris, and gases from Earth's interior reach the surface. The formation of a volcano begins when magma first breaks through the surface of Earth and erupts as lava. Solidifying quickly, this lava has the potential to become mountains of igneous rock.

If pressure caused by expanding gases and magma builds beneath the surface, eruptions can be explosive, potentially capable of wiping out cities and towns. Other eruptions can be quiet, occurring with very little consequence as soupy lava oozes from fissures and cracks within the earth.

Viscosity of Magma

The viscosity of molten rock has a lot to do with how a volcano forms and the characteristics of an eruption. **Viscosity** is a liquid's resistance to flow. Molten rock can vary in viscosity. Some is highly viscous and has the consistency of wet cement. Less viscous magma flows more easily with a consistency like running water.

The viscosity of molten rock is affected by its chemical composition and temperature. Molten rock that is high in silica produces highly viscous, light colored lava that does not flow very easily. This lava can pro-

duce granite. Molten rock having low silica content is usually darker, flows more easily, and forms rock like basalt.

The temperature of molten rock also varies largely. Higher temperatures lead to less viscous lava that flows easier than lava with lower temperatures.

Explosive Eruptions

Picture yourself blowing air through a straw into a glass of water. As gases travel from your lungs to the water, you see gas bubbles rise to the surface. As they reach the surface, the bubbles release the gas and make a small popping sound.

If you blew bubbles into a glass of mud, larger bubbles would rise to the surface. When they reached the surface, these larger bubbles would release the gas as an explosion, spreading mud in all directions.

Magma high in silica is thick and sticky like the mud in the glass. The high viscosity of this magma prevents it from releasing trapped gas as effectively as magma with lower viscosity. Trapped gas results in pressure build-up, which can lead to explosive eruptions. The explosive nature of some of these eruptions can blast solid pieces of rock and large amounts of volcanic ash thousands of meters into the air. This is often combined with a **pyroclastic flow**, which is an avalanche of gas, ash, and rock flowing down the side of a volcano, leaving destruction in its path! These kinds of eruptions are common in subduction zone volcanoes, such as at Mount St. Helens and others in the "Ring of Fire" around the Pacific Ocean.

Effusive Eruptions

Magma with low silica content is less viscous, which leads to effusive, or quiet, eruptions. These eruptions are not as explosive, as the erupting lava can flow quite easily and can continue to flow many kilometers from its source, as it does on the island of Hawai'i. Low silica magmas are called basaltic magmas which cool to form black rocks.

✓ Check for Understanding

How are fluids with high viscosity different from ones with low viscosity?

How does the viscosity of magma affect an eruption?

Where Volcanoes Form

Like earthquakes, volcanoes are often located close to plate boundaries. Countries near or on plate boundaries, like Japan, Indonesia, Iceland, and New Zealand, are prone to earthquakes, and are also host to a large number of volcanoes.

Convergent Plate Boundaries

Some volcanoes form at convergent boundaries where two plates collide. When there is a density difference between the colliding plates, usually between oceanic and continental plates, subduction can occur. The leading edge of the plate with higher density will sink below the plate of lower density and pull the plate into the hot asthenosphere.

As the descending plate reaches a depth of about 100-200 km (62-124 mi) below Earth's surface, huge temperature and pressure increases cause the plate to release a mixture of trapped water and gases. This mixture rises toward the surface and melts the lithosphere above, turning it into molten rock. This hot magma can collect below the surface and form huge **magma chambers**. Over time, these magma chambers can cool and solidify, forming **batholiths**, which can eventually become the backbone of a mountain range like the Sierra Nevada mountain range.

If the molten rock does not collect in underground magma chambers, but instead erupts as lava on Earth's surface, it forms a volcano. Over time, erupting lava and ash can gradually form large volcanic mountain ranges.

When two continental plates collide, they both tend to remain afloat. Because their density is similar and lower than the mantle below, neither plate is fully subducted. Instead, they essentially crash into one another, like two equally sized cars crashing head on. This crash crumples the two plates together, increasing the thickness of the crust at these locations. The Himalayan mountains are the result of the Indian and Eurasian continental plates colliding.

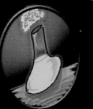

Try This!

Use an aluminum tray to represent the sea floor. Flatten out different colored discs of clay and place one on top of another until you have formed a broad shield volcano. Different colors represent extrusive igneous rock layers formed by effusive eruptions. Cut a cross-section through your volcano and observe how the layers have formed.

Repeat the procedure, but take a chunk out of bottom layers of the volcano before you add on successive layers of clay. This simulates caldera formation and the destructive energy of an explosive eruption. Cut a cross-section through this volcano, and compare the layering patterns of explosive and effusive volcanic eruptions.

Consider how islands are formed in the ocean by these kinds of volcanic processes on the sea floor. How would islands formed from effusive eruptions differ from those formed by explosive eruptions?

In some regions of the world, two oceanic plates of different densities will collide, resulting in the subduction of the plate with higher density. This subduction results in deep ocean trenches, such as the Mariana Trench east of the Philippines. Challenger Deep, the deepest known point of Earth's oceans, plunges about 11,000 m (6.8 mi) into the ocean—a depth that could fit Mount Everest and still have 2 km (1.2 mi) to spare! These plate collisions can also form a string of **volcanic islands** called an **island arc**. Examples of island arcs include the Mariana Islands, Japan, the Aleutians, and the Lesser Antillies.

Divergent Plate Boundaries

When two tectonic plates move apart, volcanic mountain ranges, like the mid-ocean ridge, can form. As plates diverge, the rock layers are placed under tension forces which cause rock layers to thin. Imagine pulling a piece of clay from both ends. The clay stretches and gradually thins near the middle.

Molten rock below the surface can melt through this thinning layer and erupt to the surface, forming volcanic ridges. The hydrothermal vents first discovered by Dr. Ballard and his team are closely associated with these volcanic ridges.

Hot Spots

If you were to drain the entire Pacific Ocean of its water, you would uncover the long and winding mid-ocean ridge, deep and dark trenches, and towering volcanoes. Volcanoes tall enough to pierce the ocean's surface are known as volcanic islands. Volcanic islands include such places as Hawai'i and Tonga.

You would also uncover many smaller volcanoes, called seamounts, rising up from the ocean floor. The appearance of many islands and seamounts occurring away from plate boundaries suggests to scientists that they may be caused by **hot spots,** or localized regions of magma close to the crust's surface.

At these hot spots, currents or plumes of heat are thought to rise from the mantle, melting rock under the crust and turning it into magma. As magma rises, it

Example

The Hawaiian Islands formed as plate movement pulled a growing volcano off a hot spot. This cut off the supply of lava to that volcano; however, another volcano would form nearby. Over time, a chain of islands appeared in the direction of the plate movement.

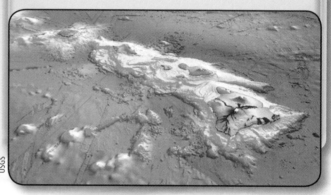

USGS

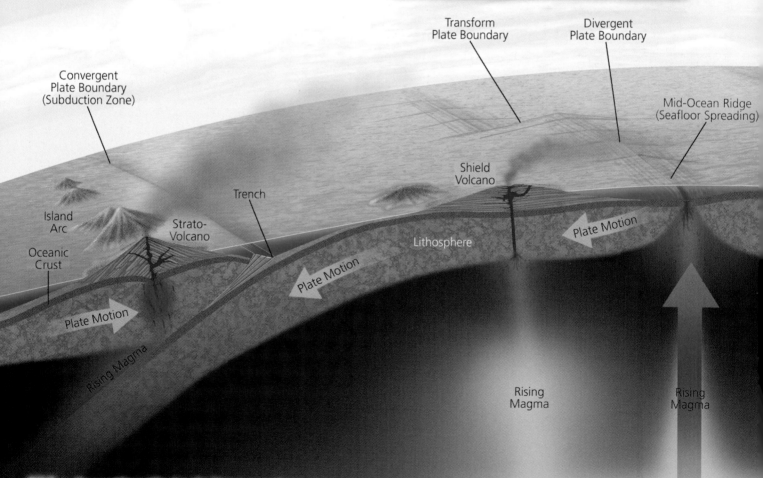

melts its way through the solid crust and erupts as lava. Over time, the cycle of eruption, cooling, and solidification can form underwater seamounts. In some cases, the volcanic source can persist for millions of years, gradually forming volcanoes high enough to break through to the ocean's surface, forming islands like Hawai'i.

Volcanic islands can be easy to navigate around because we can see them. However, there are thousands of undiscovered seamounts scattered around our oceans. Dr. Walter Smith's ocean floor maps are helping to uncover these obstacles, providing safe passageways for ships and submarines.

Geothermal Activity

Regions where volcanoes are found are often associated with **geothermal activity**. Geothermal activity occurs as magma rises to the surface and heats rocks in the crust. These rocks may contain groundwater which also gets heated. Heated water expands, causing pressure to build up around the surrounding rock. The pressure pushes the hot water up through cracks, moving it to the surface.

Hot water near the surface is a great source of renewable energy. It can warm the ground and even heat to a boil, as seen in some regions of Iceland and Japan, and in Yellowstone National Park. Geothermal activity can also form hot pools of water, hot lakes, and even hot springs. Sometimes, it can emerge with enough force to produce **geysers**, or jets of hot water and steam that shoot into the air from a vent in the ground.

Deep underground, minerals within the heated rock can sometimes dissolve into the hot water that is brought to the surface. When this occurs, minerals that once were deep inside Earth can be redistributed around the edges of hot springs as minerals precipitate out from the cooling solution.

✓ Check for Understanding

Where do volcanoes occur?

How were the Hawaiian Islands formed?

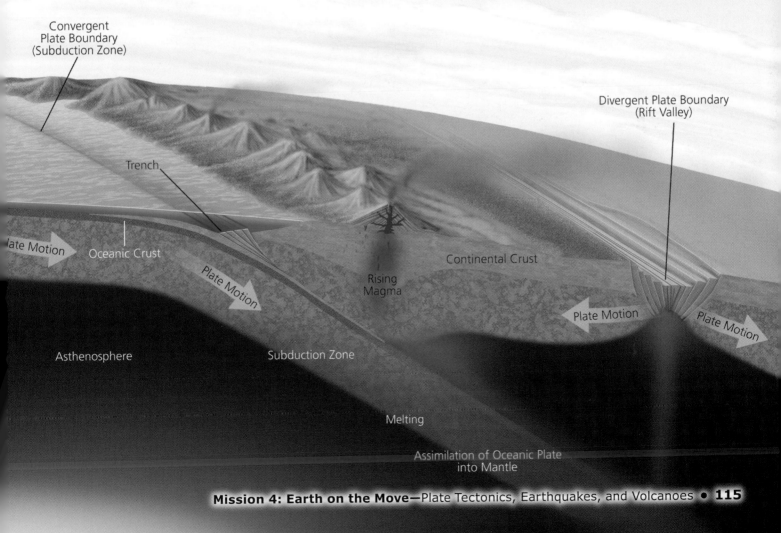

Convergent Plate Boundary (Subduction Zone)

Divergent Plate Boundary (Rift Valley)

Trench

Plate Motion

Oceanic Crust

Plate Motion

Continental Crust

Rising Magma

Plate Motion

Plate Motion

Asthenosphere

Subduction Zone

Melting

Assimilation of Oceanic Plate into Mantle

Lava Formations

As material that was once inside Earth explodes or oozes to the surface through vents or cracks in Earth's crust, land formations are created. Lava, ash, and rocks delivered to the surface can gradually become giant volcanic mountains, islands, or eventually turn into lakes! The types of landforms produced depend upon the relationships between the location of the vents, magma composition, and plate boundaries involved.

Cinder Cone

Cinder cones form as volcanic debris and low viscosity lava erupt under pressure, sometimes like a fountain from Earth's surface. This lava can solidify quickly in the air, and over time, accumulate to form a steep, cone-shaped hill.

Shield

Shields form as effusive eruptions from low viscosity lava cool and solidify. Over time, this can produce layer upon layer of igneous rock that forms a broad base and has a gentle slope.

Composite

Composites form as high viscosity lava flows and explosive eruptions alternate. Tall and cone-shaped, the surface layers of composite volcanoes alternate between extrusive igneous rock and ash.

Caldera and Crater

Calderas form when an explosive eruption empties the magma chamber of a volcano, causing it to collapse and leave a void. Craters form from lava eruptions and the gradual build-up of extrusive igneous rock. They are circular depressions at the summit of a volcano.

Lava Plateau

Lava plateaus form as low viscosity lava flows through vents in Earth's crust. The viscosity of the lava allows it to spread out before it cools. Over time, these layers build up to form a plateau.

Magma Formations

In some cases, rising magma does not quite reach the surface, but instead, cools and solidifies underground. These sometimes massive, underground structures are revealed as overlying layers of rock gradually weather and erode away.

Batholith

Atul666/Wikimedia Commons

Batholiths form when massive amounts of magma cool and solidify underground. Unearthing these underground igneous structures can take millions of years of weathering, erosion, and tectonic uplifting of the land. The enormous size of some batholiths can form the base of mountain ranges.

Dome Mountain

Oyama No Taisho/Wikimedia Commons

Dome mountains form when pockets of high viscosity magma rise up from within Earth. This magma pushes layers of overlying sedimentary rock upwards, causing them to form a dome shape. The magma does not reach the surface, but instead cools and solidifies to form the foundation of the dome mountain.

Dike and Sill

Wingchi Poon/Wikimedia Commons

Dikes form when magma cuts across pre-existing layers of rock, cools, and solidifies. **Sills** form when magma squeezes between pre-existing horizontal layers of rock, cools, and then solidifies. Weathering and erosion of overlying rock layers work to expose these structures.

tarotastic/Wikimedia Commons

Volcanic Neck

Amcaja/Wikimedia Commons

Volcanic necks form as cooling magma solidifies underground in the pipe-like channels that supply volcanoes with magma. As igneous rock is often harder than overlying sedimentary layers, sedimentary layers weather and erode away exposing typically jagged tooth-like structures.

Volcanic Consequences

Picture yourself on a volcanic island paradise surrounded by lush landscape teeming with the sounds and colors of life. Stretching as far as the eye can see is an ecosystem nourished by soil that has developed over millions of years of volcanic activity.

Volcanic eruptions are essential for allowing material that was once stored inside Earth to reach the surface. Rich and fertile volcanic soil helps to support life on Earth, but the fury and power of some eruptions can also cause devastation. That is why it is important to understand the fine balance between the advantages and limitations of living near volcanoes.

Living Near Volcanoes

When a volcano erupts, it can result in lava flows. This lava can reach over 1,000°C (1,832°F), burning almost everything in its path! However, lava does not always flow along the ground; it can also be ejected into the sky. As it cools and solidifies in the air, it can rain down boulders of volcanic rock. Heat released by eruptions can also instantly melt snow which can turn soil into mudflows that strip mountains and valleys bare. This occurred on Mount St. Helens in 1980.

Sometimes, that is just the beginning. Volcanic eruptions can also expel large amounts of ash and toxic fumes. Breathing in ash and toxic gases is sometimes the most deadly part of an eruption, and can cause lung damage or suffocation.

Volcano Preparedness

If you happen to live near a volcano or are visiting an area with volcanoes, it might be helpful to know whether the volcanoes are active, dormant, or extinct. An extinct volcano is one that will not erupt again. Dormant volcanoes show very little signs of volcanic activity, but may erupt in the future. Unlike a dormant or an extinct volcano, active volcanoes show signs that they are preparing to erupt. These include the release of

Example

Ash produced by volcanoes can be dangerous. An explosive volcanic eruption on April 14, 2010, under the Eyjafjallajökull glacier in Iceland, created a massive cloud of volcanic ash that covered most of northern Europe. The presence of volcanic ash in the atmosphere made it too dangerous to fly in many parts of Europe, causing over 100,000 flights to be cancelled world-wide, and costing airlines about $1.7 billion in revenue. Particles of volcanic ash ejected by an eruption can severely damage jet engines. Abrasion by ash can damage windshields and result in zero visibility for pilots.

Boaworm/Wikimedia Commons

steam and gas from vents, usually indicating that pressure within the volcano may be increasing due to rising levels of magma.

If you do live in an area that is known for volcanic activity, you might want to be prepared with a volcano emergency kit. Recommended items include goggles, masks, a radio, a flashlight, and plenty of extra batteries. Residents living near volcanoes should also be aware of evacuation routes and procedures.

If a Volcano Erupts

If a volcano does erupt in your area, use your radio to get information about safe evacuation routes. These routes will steer you clear of lava, mudflows, and flying rocks and debris. Before you evacuate, put on long sleeves and long pants to protect your skin. Wear goggles and cover your mouth with a wet cloth or mask to avoid breathing in toxic fumes.

Volcanic ash can also damage property. Prevent ash from entering your house by closing windows and doors, and blocking chimneys. Eruptions like these do not happen every day and are usually very rare events. However, they are unavoidable and important reminders for all to respect the beauty and awesome power of our ever-changing planet.

✓ Check for Understanding

Why might people want to live near a volcano?

USGS

Viscosity and Volcanoes

Before Walter Smith began mapping the ocean floor, it was not known how many underwater volcanoes existed. Some people even speculated that there were not many volcanoes the size of the ones we see on the land. By using the data from satellites, Walter has found that there are many volcanoes throughout the oceans, and some of them are the same size as or larger than ones on land. Just as we see with land volcanoes, these ocean volcanoes have distinct shapes that are most likely associated with the magma which erupts from them and the plate boundaries with which they are associated.

In this activity, you will experiment with a variety of variables that affect the composition and viscosity of simulated magma. From your experiments, you will predict the effect of the magma viscosity on the volcano shape it would produce. Then, you will identify locations in the world where similar volcanoes exist and the plate boundaries with which they are associated.

Materials
- Lab 3 Data Sheet
- sugar
- water
- thermometer
- graduated cylinder
- beaker
- sand
- soil mixtures
- containers
- ruler
- masking tape
- large board of plastic or wood
- stopwatch
- supports
- food coloring

Lab Prep

1. Set up the elevated ramp and collection container as shown in the data sheet.

2. Measure 25 mL of water. Add a few drops of food coloring and record the temperature. This represents Lava A.

3. At the starting line, gently pour the 25 mL of water and time how long it takes for it to first get to the finish line. Repeat two more times, and average all three trials.

4. Repeat step 3 with Lava B, composed of sugar and water, provided by your teacher.

Make Observations

1. Design an experiment to investigate how different variables, such as temperature or composition, affect viscosity or the flow of Lava B. Share your experiment with your instructor for approval.

2. Conduct your experiment and report your findings to your class.

3. Based on your data, predict which lava solution will flow furthest from the volcano before solidifying. Which lava would not flow very far before it solidifies? What is the relationship between lava viscosity and distance traveled?

4. Based on the hypothetical distance of each solution or lava flow, describe the potential effects of higher or lower viscosity lava on the formation of a volcano after multiple eruptions.

   a. Which would produce a volcano with a large base and gentle slopes? Why?

   b. Which would produce a volcano with a smaller base and very steep slopes? Why?

5. Analyze the pictures in the data sheet to determine whether the volcanoes may have high or low viscosity lava.

6. Use the Smithsonian's Global Volcanism Program online to find examples and locations of each type of volcano. Using the map of plate boundaries in the data sheet, determine which type of boundary each example is associated with, and which boundaries are more likely to produce each type of volcano.

 Journal Question Describe the relationships between lava viscosity, volcano type, and plate boundaries.

Monitoring Earthquakes and Eruptions

Even though it is impossible to prevent an earthquake or volcanic eruption from happening, millions of people live in regions around the world that are prone to these natural disasters. Therefore, scientists must learn more about earthquakes and volcanoes to predict where and when they will occur. Specialized devices to monitor movement in Earth's crust provide scientists with information about changes at plate boundaries and the activity of volcanoes.

By monitoring plate movement and volcanic activity around-the-clock, scientists have noticed that earthquakes and volcanoes often provide a few hints before they strike or erupt. Usually, changes to the level or shape of the ground occur. These changes are caused by stress building up in layers of rock caused as plates push against one another at a fault. It can also be caused as magma rises and fills a volcano's magma chamber. The change in volume caused by the magma can exert tremendous pressure upon the walls within the volcano resulting in a bulge. These surface changes are closely monitored so scientists can predict the location and magnitude of an earthquake or the extent to which a volcano may erupt.

Tilt Meters

Scientists use tilt meters to detect elevation changes of the land. Tilt meters work like a carpenter's level, where a bubble is placed in a tube of liquid. Any change in elevation on either side of the tube will move the bubble. The degree of tilt is recorded by how far the bubble moves. Tilt meters are usually placed near the edge of a fault or on the slope of a volcano.

Lasers

In order to detect very small surface movements, electronic distance measurements are made using lasers. A laser beam is aimed at a reflector placed some distance away, which reflects the beam back to the device. A computer calculates the distance by calculating the time it took for the laser to bounce back. Laser measurements are sensitive enough to detect land movements of just 1 mm (0.04 in.) over a distance of 1 km (0.6 mi)!

Satellites

One of the most effective ways of detecting surface changes is by remote sensing using satellites. Orbiting from such a high altitude, satellites are extremely useful tools for monitoring change because they are able to monitor Earth's surface on a wide scale.

Satellites equipped with imaging radar can detect changes in the elevation and tilt of the ground surface, and have mapped changes caused by earthquakes and volcanoes. Ground-based receivers of **Global Positioning System (GPS)** satellite navigation signals can monitor the direction in which plates move. This gives scientists, like Dr. Walter Smith, a more complete understanding of the mechanisms driving plate tectonics and the different interactions between plates.

Satellites can also be equipped with temperature sensors, which monitor Earth's surface temperature changes. Temperature increases detected in surface layers of rock near a volcano are usually the result of magma rising, a sign that a volcano is about to erupt. Volcanic activity can also be monitored using sensors that detect the release of ash and gas by volcanoes.

Jason-2 Satellite

Orbiting Earth as part of the Ocean Surface Topography Mission (OSTM), the Jason-2 Satellite provides a rich array of data for scientists studying weather, climate, ocean currents, wave heights, and sea levels. Dr. Walter Smith uses this state-of-the-art satellite, which is a joint effort between NASA and the French Space Agency, to determine the location and size of underwater land masses like volcanoes, trenches, and seamounts directly beneath the satellite's orbit.

Orbit Radius: 7,714 km (4,793 mi)

Altitude at Equator: 1,336 km (830 mi)

Obit Inclination: 66 degrees (orbit path ranges from 66 degrees north to 66 degrees south)

Orbit Time: 6,745.72 seconds

Communication: Two-way S Band microwaves for data transmission on corkscrew antennas

Radar Frequencies: 12.6 GHz to measure the ocean surface and 5.3 GHz to measure interference from electrons and water vapor in the atmosphere

Data collection is about 1,000 times faster than ship-based sonar. The 1.6 km (1 mi) measurement zone and 315 km (196 mi) gaps between measurement orbits are still large enough to hide volcanoes and seamounts. To find these features, Walter adds in data collected by the Geosat and ERS-1 satellites, which reduces the data gaps to about 4 km (2.5 mi), and allows Dr. Smith to create maps of the ocean floor of the entire world.

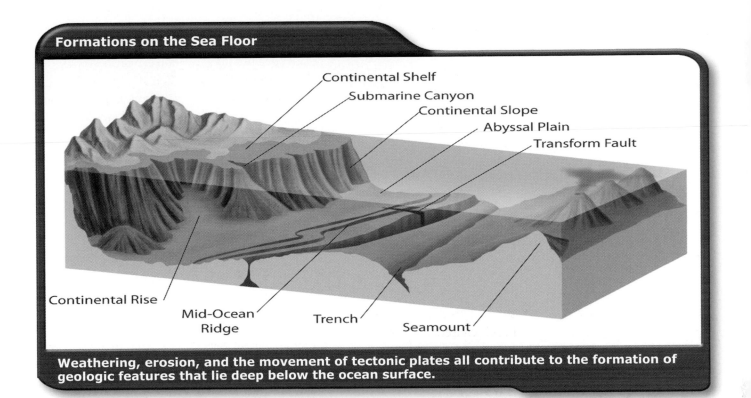

Formations on the Sea Floor

- Continental Shelf
- Submarine Canyon
- Continental Slope
- Abyssal Plain
- Transform Fault
- Continental Rise
- Mid-Ocean Ridge
- Trench
- Seamount

Weathering, erosion, and the movement of tectonic plates all contribute to the formation of geologic features that lie deep below the ocean surface.

Seismographic Data

Because a large proportion of earthquakes and eruptions occur near faults, which are tectonic boundaries, it is important for geologists to determine where boundaries are located. Some are easy to see, like parts the San Andreas Fault on the west coast of North America or the Great Rift Valley in northeastern Africa. Others are buried under layers of rock, soil, and water, or are hidden by dense vegetation.

Seismographs can be used to detect these hidden boundaries by detecting and measuring the reflection of seismic waves. When seismic waves encounter boundaries, such as faults, they reflect. By locating areas where these reflections occur, scientists can map the depth and length of these boundaries.

Monitoring seismic activity can also reveal areas along faults that have very little seismic activity compared to other areas along the fault. One might think that an area around a fault that did not have much seismic activity would be safe. However, the absence of earthquakes can indicate that the plate boundaries are "stuck," and if they become "unstuck," they could unleash a powerful earthquake.

Undersea Mapping

Dr. Walter Smith's sea-floor mapping work also provides us with valuable knowledge about earthquakes and volcanoes. His maps help scientists predict potential locations for earthquakes, tsunamis, and undersea volcanic eruptions. Using Walter's maps, scientists can estimate the motion of plates and the potential magnitude of earthquakes in certain regions of the world by identifying the plate boundaries. They can also use his maps to identify the many volcanoes hidden beneath hundreds, and even thousands, of meters of water.

Creating maps of the ocean floor, studying the direction and speed in which plates move, and monitoring earthquakes and volcanoes are helping us better understand the dynamic nature of our world. The application of the knowledge we gain from these scientific studies is also helping to protect people and property around the world.

✔ Check for Understanding

Why is it important to monitor plate boundaries?

Exploring Our Oceans

Recall that your mission is *to journey through the oceans and Earth's outer layers to its core to better understand the dynamic nature of our planet*. Now that you have been fully briefed, it is time to analyze data and maps of volcanoes, earthquakes, and ocean floor topography throughout the world.

Since around 70 percent of Earth's surface is covered with water and is difficult to explore, much about the ocean floor is still relatively unknown. So, Walter Smith is trying to map and explore the entire ocean floor. To do so, he uses the Jason-2 and other satellites that measure changes in the height of the ocean surface caused by the gravity of the sea-floor geology below the surface. In fact, most of the oceans' geologic features currently presented in Google Earth™ are largely the result of Walter's satellite research and data. He hopes to make higher resolution maps as we explore the ocean with more advanced technologies.

One goal of Dr. Smith's research is to map all of the seamounts on the ocean floor. Some of these seamounts are currently volcanically active, while many are old and not active. Knowing where the seamounts are located is just the first step in this research. The next step, determining whether they are active or not, is difficult. Some ways include listening for eruptions with listening arrays on boats, detecting earthquakes on or under the seamount, or diving down in a submersible to film an eruption or find evidence of a recent lava flow. Dr. Smith is helping to guide this future research with his maps, which can further develop our understanding of the volcanic and tectonic history of Earth.

In this activity, you will analyze a map of a section of the Pacific Northwest which contains information on recently active volcanoes and probable seamounts identified by Walter Smith. You will then compare this map data to earthquake data in this region to recommend probable seamounts for further study. Once you have completed this analysis, you will explore other areas around the world to identify locations that could potentially contain active undocumented volcanoes.

Materials

- **Mission 4 Field Assignment Data Sheet**
- **computer with Internet access and Google Earth™ installed**

Objectives:

- Analyze data of recently active volcanoes, probable seamounts, ocean floor topography, and earthquakes in a section of the Pacific Northwest.

- Develop and defend a recommendation for which seamounts should be researched further.

- Use mapping tools, such as Google Earth™, to collect data on other areas around the world that experience volcanic and earthquake activity.

- Work together as a class to determine areas around the world that should be focused on to further develop our understanding of the volcanic and tectonic history of Earth.

Field Prep

1 Analyze the map in the data sheet which includes the following data:

  a. Volcanoes marked as recently active volcanoes by the Smithsonian's Global Volcanism Program (GVP). This project documents all known active volcanoes and their eruptions during the last 10,000 years.

  b. Volcanoes marked as probable seamounts by Dr. Smith. The volcanic activity of these features has not been determined, though many are presumed to be extinct.

2 Determine the number of recently active volcanoes that were verified by the GVP on the map.

3 Determine the number of probable seamounts identified by Walter Smith on the map.

4 What percentage of the identified features on the ocean floor are classified as active volcanoes? What percentage are classified as probable seamounts?

5 Develop a hypothesis as to why the two percentages identified in step 4 are different.

6 Describe the geologic topography and landforms at and around the recently active volcanoes and probable seamounts.

7 Describe the distribution of the active and probable locations on the land and in the ocean. Do there seem to be any patterns in their distribution? If so, explain.

8 Analyze the USGS map of earthquake activity in this region.

9 Compare and contrast the earthquake locations map to the locations of the probable seamounts. Since earthquake activity under or around a probable seamount may be an indicator that it is active, determine any seamounts or groups of seamounts that would be good candidates for further research. Defend your answer.

10 Share and compare your results with your class.

Mission Challenge

Your mission is to identify areas of the ocean or land that could potentially contain undocumented active volcanoes based on currently known volcanoes, earthquake data, topography, and the location of tectonic plates.

1 Open Google Earth™. Turn on the Volcano and Earthquake layers within the Places of Interest or Gallery layer folders. You can also download the USGS layer of recent earthquake activity and plate boundaries from the JMC.

2 Locate the Pacific Northwest region which you have been analyzing using Dr. Smith's map. Zoom into different areas of this region to further your analysis of the volcanoes, earthquakes, and topography of this area. Even though many of the probable seamounts identified on Dr. Smith's map are not identified in Google Earth™, describe the sea-floor topography at and around the seamounts in this region.

3 Locate two to three areas in the ocean or on land which have volcanic activity that you would like to study further.

4 Determine the type and elevation of the volcanoes in each area you have selected to research. Click on each icon on the map to get more information.

5 Zoom into these areas to analyze the earthquake activity around each research area.

6 Click on some of the earthquakes to determine the date of occurrence, magnitude, and depth.

7 If you have downloaded the USGS layer from the JMC, determine the location of the nearest plate boundary and the locations of any recent earthquakes in your research area.

8 Analyze the ocean floor topography around your research areas to identify any features which could be probable seamounts. Compare these to the seamounts on the map in the Field Prep.

Mission Debrief

1 Using the locations of earthquake activity, current volcano activity, ocean floor topography, and plate boundary location, identify specific locations that may contain undocumented volcanoes.

2 Make a recommendation for each potential study site.

3 Share your recommendations with your class.

4 Aggregate and analyze all group recommendations and rationale for studying each.

5 Determine which recommendations and rationale may provide the best location for starting further research.

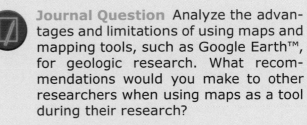

Journal Question Analyze the advantages and limitations of using maps and mapping tools, such as Google Earth™, for geologic research. What recommendations would you make to other researchers when using maps as a tool during their research?

Picture yourself on a beach. Soft white sand rubs between your toes as you hear the hypnotic sound of waves beating against the shore. Peering out over the seemingly endless ocean, you can barely tell where the ocean ends and sky begins. Slipping into the water and paddling out on your surfboard, there's no other place you'd rather be.

THE GEOLOGY OF SURFING

Surfing has become a large part of society in many parts of the world. Both old and new movies, such as *The Endless Summer* and *Surf's Up*, and clothing lines, such as Quiksilver™, Roxy™, and Billabong™, were created because of the cultural fascination with surfing. Peppered along thousands of miles of coastline are surf communities that thrive on riding good waves. But, what makes a good wave? Whether they realize it or not, surfers gather because of geology.

Many experts believe that the birthplace of surfing is Hawai'i. Luckily for surfers, the process that formed the islands of Hawai'i provided just the right slope for ocean swells to break upon Hawai'i's shores. One of the world's most famous surf breaks is located on the North Shore of Oahu, Hawai'i. Named after its tubular shape, Pipeline has challenged some of the best surfers in the world.

Indonesia is another prime location where surfers flock to ride near perfect waves. The island arc of Indonesia is comprised of over 17,000 islands. The western half of the country formed as the Indian plate subducted under the Eurasian plate. Approximately 100-200 kilometers (62-124 miles) below the ocean

DID YOU KNOW?

Surfing is strongly rooted in Hawaiian culture. Royalty trained as surfers because wave riding skill was believed to indicate one's ability to lead. Surfing was not just a physical pastime, it had a spiritual component as well. Hawaiians would pray to the Kahuna (priests or experts) for good waves. Spirituality also played an important role when making their ancient wooden surfboards as construction would often require extensive rituals.

Shalom Jacobovitz/Wikimedia Commons

floor, the subducting oceanic plate melted and became molten rock. This molten rock erupted as lava on the ocean floor. Very similar to the way Hawai'i formed, layers of volcanic rock built up over time to form islands. The island of Bali in Indonesia has formed in just the right angle and direction to host some of the world's best surfing waves.

Shalom Jacobovitz/Wikimedia Commons

Every once in a while, violent storms churn the seas to a point where giant waves break miles offshore on top of seamounts. Situated about 160 kilometers (100 miles) off the coast of California is the Cortes Bank, an undersea mountain range with some peaks rising to just 1.2 to 1.5 meters (4 to 5 feet) below the ocean's surface. It is home to some of the biggest waves ever ridden. When swell direction, wind, and tides are forecasted to align in just the right way, a handful of big wave surfers from around the world will gather to test their skills against the ocean's fury. Some surfers get help from jet skiers to catch these waves.

Surfers have been reaping the benefits of millions of years of tectonic activity as waves break off coastlines every single day. As we become more aware of Earth's varied coastal geology, new surf spots will continue to be discovered. Today, with access to online resources like Google Earth™ and real-time wave and weather reports, they can apply their understanding of geology to discover new surf breaks and chase waves that may have once gone un-ridden!

VOCABULARY OF SURFING

Over the years, surfers have developed slang words to describe waves, other surfers, and the feeling one gets from riding waves. Though you may not realize it, these words have become popular in everyday culture. How many of the words below have you used or have you heard used?

Amped Overdoing it; excited.

Bail Jump off your board to avoid a major wipe out.

Beached Full from eating.

Bogus False; lame; unbelievable.

Bummer Too bad; a drag.

Cowabunga A yell of excitement by a surfer (also "Banzai").

Ding A hole or dent on a surfboard.

Dude A male surfer (women surfers are called "dudettes").

Eat It To fall off of a surfboard.

Gnarly Large and dangerous.

Hot-dogging Fancy surfing.

Max Out To be over the limit.

Off the Richter Something that's very good, excellent, or "off the scale."

Rad/Radical Very good; excellent.

Sick Anything that is out of the ordinary.

Stoked Happy; excited.

Wipe Out To fall off your board.

YOUR TURN

Popular surf breaks are often the focal point of surfing towns, with surf shops, contests, and beach clean-ups, and are often featured on web cams. Use online resources to analyze a popular surfing town, and get to know the town's "personality." What makes it a surfing town? What geologic landforms nearby create great surfing waves? How did the community develop over the years? What describes the culture of the town? Using your research, create an advertisement to encourage tourists to visit your surfing town.

Join the Argonaut Adventure!

Work with and learn from the greatest explorers, scientists, and researchers in the world as they engage in today's most exciting scientific explorations. JASON is always looking for Argonauts to join our science adventure. Find out here how you can be part of the team!

▲ JASON researchers share their work, their inspirations, and their passion with students in JASON Live Events.

Interact with JASON Argonauts

The **JASON Mission Center** is your gateway to meeting the JASON National Argonauts from *Operation: Tectonic Fury*. Log into the **JASON Mission Center**, click **Message Boards**, ask the Argos a question, and they will be happy to respond! You will also be able to discuss JASON with other students from around the world. You can also follow the Argonauts adventures through their captivating bios, journals, and photo galleries.

YOU ARE AN ARGONAUT TOO!

What are your interests? What would you want to tell other people about yourself? What do you like most about your JASON experience and being part of the JASON community?

Join a JASON Live Event

JASON gives you a chance to ask questions of scientists and watch them answer—live! With live demonstrations, polls, and interactivity, JASON Live Events will light the spark of inspiration in your classroom. Visit the JASON Mission Center and click **Live Events** to learn more.

▲ Students have many opportunities to get more information from the Argonauts and other experts and personal answers to their questions through the message boards and live, online events.

National Argonauts

Interested in becoming a National Argonaut yourself and working with the next group of JASON Host Researchers? Check online often to learn about the next opportunity and how to apply!

Begin your Argonaut Adventure at *www.jason.org*

Each year JASON recruits a team of expert scientists, students, and teachers to serve on our Missions. To learn more about the Host Researchers, log into the JASON Mission Center to read their bios and view the Meet the Researcher videos.

Student Argonauts

CONNOR BEBB
Traverse City, MI
Mission 1, Mission 3

Connor is on the Ranger Rick youth advisory board, helping to suggest articles and giving his opinions to the editors and writers.

BEN BRANNAN
Columbus, OH
Mission 2, Mission 4

Ben is an avid soccer fan. He is very interested in science and engineering and is on his school's Science Olympiad team.

KARINA JOUGLA
Carpinteria, CA
Mission 2, Mission 4

Karina is very active in local theater and her school's student government. She is especially interested in biotechnology and how DNA can be manipulated to improve our lives.

EMILY JUDAH
College Station, TX
Mission 1, Mission 3

Emily is very active in her 4-H club with horseback riding. Emily developed the concept behind MasterMines, available in the JASON Mission Center in Fall 2010.

MARIA MARQUEZ
Monterrey, Mexico
Mission 1, Mission 3

Maria is very involved in Cadena (Girl Scouts) in her home town, and has played basketball for the past 8 years.

SACHI SANGHAVI
New Delhi, India
Mission 2, Mission 4

Sachi is interested in engineering and plans to study in the United States. She has hiked in the Himalayan mountains, which was excellent preparation for her experience on Mount St. Helens.

Teacher Argonauts

CINDY DUGUAY
Turner, ME
Mission 1, Mission 3

Cindy teaches gifted and talented students at all levels. She loves the outdoors, including skiing and hiking, and is learning how to SCUBA dive.

JENNIFER PEGLOW
Gardners, PA
Mission 2

Jennifer started her career as a language arts teacher, but is now a science teacher. She is very interested in using educational technologies to spark students' learning.

JODI PHIPPS
Salamander Bay, Australia
Mission 2, Mission 4

Jodi has taught science for over 18 years and is currently working on her certificate for teaching gifted students. In her spare time, she is an avid netball player.

Host Researchers

DR. MIKE WISE
Geologist, The Smithsonian Institution

While taking his first geology course, Mike spent his spring vacation in a pegmatite mine collecting rocks and minerals. Mike is now the curator of the pegmatite exhibit at the Smithsonian Institution's National Museum of Natural History.

DR. VIRGINIA DALE
Director, Center for BioEnergy Sustainability
Oak Ridge National Laboratory

Virginia defended her Ph.D. thesis on the same day Mount St. Helens erupted over 30 years ago. Virginia uses her mathematics and science background to determine what kinds of plants to use for biofuel production and where to cultivate them.

DR. GEORGE GUTHRIE
Focus Area Leader, Geosciences
National Energy Technology Laboratory

Before coming to NETL, George was a geologist working on the United States' efforts to store nuclear waste at Yucca Mountain. George now researches how different gases and fluids can be stored in rocks and minerals.

DR. WALTER SMITH
Geophysicist, NOAA

Walter's work with satellites has revealed thousands of new ocean floor features. Walter was instrumental in providing data for ocean features shown in Google Maps™.

Build a Soil Sieve

Assembly

1. Cut the bottom out of three pie pans.

2. Measure and cut out one piece of each screening gauge to fit over the bottom of the three cut pie pans.

3. Tape one gauge of screening over the opening on the bottom of one of the pie pans cut in Step 1. Repeat for each cut pie pan.

4. Measure the size of the openings on each screen. Mark each pan with the measured screen size.

5. Organize the pans, placing the one with the largest gauge screening on top, then second largest below, then smallest gauge, and the uncut pan on the bottom.

In the Field

1. Measure and pour your soil sample into the top pan, and shake the pan over the pan below it until all of the particles that are smaller than the screening have passed through. Set aside the top pan and its contents. Repeat this procedure shaking the soil through the remaining pans, until you get to the bottom pan.

2. Measure and record the mass of material left in each pan. Using these measurements, determine the percentage of the original soil sample that is left in each pan.

Andre Radloff/The JASON Project

Build a Soil Coring Tool

Assembly

1. Using a ruler and marker, mark the side of the PVC pipe at 1-cm increments. Mark the end 0 cm and label every other mark for reference. The end marked 0 cm is the bottom.

In the Field

1. To take a soil core, place the bottom of the PVC pipe on the ground. Place the piece of wood on the top of the PVC pipe, and carefully hammer the PVC pipe 15-20 cm into the ground. Use the markings on the side of the pipe to determine the depth of the pipe.

2. Twist the pipe to loosen it, and slowly pull the pipe out of the ground.

3. Push the dowel into the top of the PVC pipe to push the soil core out of the pipe onto a piece of white paper or cardboard.

4. Analyze the soil core:

   a. Measure the depth of different layers.

   b. Describe any color changes as you go down into the ground.

   c. Look for anything living in the soil.

5. Draw a picture of the sample and then break it up to conduct other analyses on the different parts of the profile.

Build a Soil Permeability Tool

Materials
- plastic soda/water bottle (12-20 oz, 1 L, or 2 L)
- window screening
- scissors
- ruler
- marker
- stopwatch
- graduated cylinder
- tape

Assembly

1. Cut the bottle in half.

2. Cover and tape the window screening over the inside or outside of the bottle top.

3. Using a graduated cylinder, measure 10 mL of water and pour it into the bottom half of the bottle (be sure the bottle is resting on a flat surface).

4. Using a permanent marker and water level as a guide, label the location of the water level 10 mL.

5. Add another 10 ml to the bottle and label the water level as 20 mL.

6. Repeat this several times until you have determined the total value in milliliters of each mark on the side of the bottle bottom.

In the Field

1. To test the permeability and water holding capacity of your soil sample, fill the inverted bottle top with screen with your soil sample. With the bottle opening facing down, place it over the bottom of the bottle.

2. Pour a measured amount of water onto the soil and start a stopwatch or note the time on a watch.

3. To determine the permeability, use the lines on the side of the bottle bottom to determine how long it takes for a predetermined amount of water to flow through the sample. Continue monitoring until water stops flowing out of the soil or the time limit indicated by your teacher has been reached.

4. To determine the water holding capacity of the soil, measure the total amount of water that flowed through the soil. Subtract this amount from the original amount of water poured into the soil.

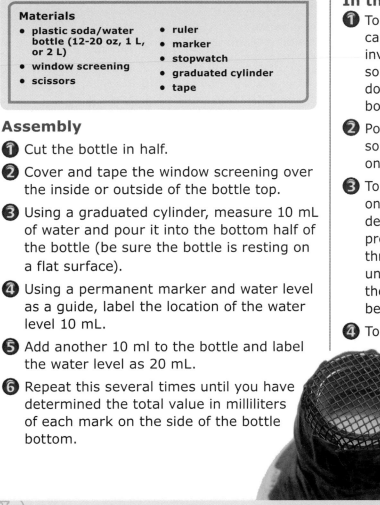

Andre Radloff/The JASON Project

Build a Soil Infiltration Tool

Materials
- empty soup/coffee can
- can opener
- permanent marker
- graduated cylinder
- rubber mallet/hammer
- piece of wood
- ruler
- stopwatch

Assembly

1. Use a can opener to cut both tops off the can.

2. Mark the outside of the can with lines spaced at 1-cm increments with zero at the bottom.

In the Field

1. Determine and clear the soil area you wish to study outside.

2. Hammer one side of the metal tube at least 2-3 cm into the ground. Use the markings on the side of the can to guide you. Use a piece of wood placed on top of the can while hammering in hard soils, to prevent denting.

3. Pour a measured amount of water into the can and time how long it takes for all of the water to absorb into the ground, eliminating all puddles.

4. If you observe water leaking out of the side, your results may be skewed. In that case, find a new test area and hammer the can deeper into the ground and try again for more accurate results.

Glossary

---A---

abrasion the scraping of rock caused by particles carried by wind, water, and ice (40)

acid rain precipitation with a pH below 7.0 due to atmospheric pollutants, such as dissolved carbon dioxide (41)

alluvial fan a deposit of sediment that spreads out onto a plain or valley floor by fast flowing water from a narrow canyon or valley (53)

anticline upward folding of layers of rock that look similar to a bowl-like concave downwards shape (71)

asthenosphere a semi-solid layer of Earth located just below the lithosphere that yields to high temperature and pressure by slowly flowing and shifting over time (98)

atom the basic component of matter consisting of protons, neutrons, and electrons (15, 74)

---B---

batholith a large mass of igneous rock with an exposed area of more than 100 square km (40 square miles) formed from the cooling of molten rock below the surface (113, 117)

beach an accumulation of sediment deposited along a shoreline (53)

bedrock the solid layer of rock in a soil profile that lies beneath loose surface material (48)

biologic sedimentary rock a type of sedimentary rock that forms from plant or animal remains (25)

butte an isolated hill with a flat top and steep sloping side, usually formed from further weathering and erosion of a mesa (53)

---C---

caldera a large depression left after a volcano erupts and the magma chamber collapses on itself (116)

carbon capture and sequestration (CCS) the collection, storage, and disposal of carbon dioxide gas that would otherwise be released into the atmosphere by processes, such as the burning of fossil fuels for energy (69)

carbon film fossil a carbon-rich remnant of a plant or animal that appears like a flat two-dimensional imprint (81)

carbonation a process where carbon dioxide (CO_2) dissolves in water (H_2O), forming carbonic acid (H_2CO_3) (41)

cast a preserved replica of an organism's outer features formed by the crystallization of minerals within a mold (80)

cementation a step in the lithification process where minerals dissolved in solution fill open pore spaces between sediment granules and re-crystallize, binding the individual grains together (25)

chemical sedimentary rock a type of sedimentary rock that forms from minerals that precipitate from solution (25)

chemical weathering a process which changes materials, such as rocks, by altering the chemical composition of its components (39)

cinder cone volcano a steep conical hill formed by volcanic debris and the solidification and accumulation of low viscous lava and volcanic debris erupting under pressure (116)

clastic sedimentary rock a type of sedimentary rock that forms from the accumulation of rock fragments and minerals (25)

cleavage the physical property of how a mineral breaks or fractures (16)

climate the average condition of the weather in a region over a period of years, as described by its range of temperature, winds, humidity, and precipitation (46)

compaction a step in the lithification process that occurs as the weight of overlying material compresses buried sediment (25)

composite volcano typically a tall, conical-shaped volcano, built up over time by eruptions of lava and volcanic debris (116)

compression force the squeezing of surface rocks that can typically cause rock layers to fold or create reverse faults (105)

compression wave a type of mechanical wave in which matter in the medium moves back and forth in the same direction that the wave travels (106)

conductivity the measure of a material's ability to transfer energy, such as thermal or electrical energy (16)

contact metamorphism occurs when heat introduced by molten rock alters minerals within a rock (27)

continental drift a theory that continents do not remain stationary but slowly move over time (97)

convection the transfer of heat energy that occurs by the flow of material (97)

convergent boundary the region where two tectonic plates move into one another (102)

core the innermost layer of Earth composed of a liquid outer core and a solid inner core (99)

cove a sheltered bay along a shoreline (53)

crater a bowl-shaped pit found at the summit of a volcano (116)

creep the slow movement of soil and rock down a slope (50)

crust the thin and solid outermost layer of Earth that is rocky with relatively low density (98)

crystal a solid with a highly uniform atomic structure (15)

crystal structure formed by the geometric pattern created by the arrangement of atoms or molecules of a mineral (15)

crystallization the formation and growth of minerals from a liquid or a gas (19)

---D---

decomposition a process where organic material is broken down by organisms such as bacteria and fungi (78)

deflation the gradual removal of loose surface material by wind resulting in shallow depressions (49)

delta a fan-shaped deposit that forms when a river or stream reaches a large body of water and releases its sediment (52)

density a physical property of matter measured by the ratio of its mass to its volume (16)

deposition the accumulation of sediment in a particular location (47)

dike an igneous intrusion that has cut across layers of pre-existing rock (117)

divergent boundary the region where two tectonic plates move away from one another (102)

dome mountain a magma formation that occurs when magma rises and solidifies underground causing overlying sedimentary rock layers to bulge (117)

drumlin an elongated mound of sediment deposited and shaped by a glacier (52)

dune a hill or mound created by wind deposition of sand (49)

---E---

earthquake sudden movements of Earth's crust usually occurring along active plate boundaries (104)

eon the largest unit of geologic time (84)

epicenter the location on Earth's surface situated directly above an earthquake's focus (106)

epoch a unit of geologic time that subdivides periods (85)

era a unit of geologic time, based upon the general types of organisms that existed on Earth during these times. It is smaller than an eon and includes several periods (85)

erosion the process of moving sediment from one place to another, usually by wind, water, gravity, or a combination of these factors (38, 47)

eruption a phenomenon that occurs when molten rock and volcanic gases and debris from Earth's interior reach the surface (112)

evaporate a change of state from liquid to gas, caused by the gain of heat energy in the liquid (19)

exfoliation a mechanical weathering process that occurs when outer layers of rock flake off (40)

extrusion lava that erupts, flows, and solidifies on top of pre-existing rock formations (72)

extrusive rock a type of igneous rock that forms on or very near Earth's surface as lava cools and solidifies (24)

─────────────── F ───────────────

fault a break in Earth's crust caused by the movement of one side of the break relative to the other (72, 104)

felsic rocks and minerals that form from molten rock rich in silicon dioxide molecules (19, 98)

fjord a U-shaped valley eroded by a glacier and filled with seawater (48)

fin a long thin sedimentary rock feature that over time, can weather and erode to become a hoodoo (53)

focus the location beneath Earth's surface from which an earthquake originates (106)

fold a rock layer feature where a layer of rock doubles up or bends, usually by compression forces (104)

foliated metamorphic rock a type of metamorphic rock formed when minerals within pre-existing rock are squeezed flat or elongated resulting in a banded layered appearance often reflecting the direction the pressure was applied (27)

fossil remains or traces of organisms preserved in Earth's crust (78)

fossil record a chronological list of life forms that existed in Earth's past (82)

─────────────── G ───────────────

gemstone a crystalline mineral that can be beautiful, rare, durable, and is sometimes worn as jewelry after being cut and polished (22)

geologic time a time scale representing the physical formation and development of life on Earth which can be divided by eons, eras, periods, and epochs (84)

geology the study of Earth and its history as recorded in rocks and minerals (7)

geothermal activity the heating of material on or near Earth's surface by energy within Earth (115)

geyser a jet of hot water and steam that occasionally erupts from a vent in the ground (115)

glacier a large, long-lived accumulation of ice, snow, liquid water, and sediment originating on land that moves due to the force of its mass and gravity (48)

Global Positioning System (GPS) technology that uses satellites, ground receivers, and computers to determine one's location on Earth (120)

Gondwanaland an ancient continent, originally the southern part of Pangaea, that broke up to become South America, Africa, Arabia, India, Australia, and Antarctica (97)

gravity the force of attraction that exists between any two objects (102)

groundwater water below Earth's surface that fills empty spaces in rock (47)

─────────────── H ───────────────

half-life the amount of time it takes for one-half of the mass of a radioactive isotope to decay (75)

hardness the physical property of a mineral's ability to resist scratching (16)

hoodoo a column of rock that forms as a result of a cap of hard rock that protects underlying layers from weathering and erosion (53)

hot spot a localized region of magma close to Earth's crust (114)

humus organic substance made of decayed animal or plant matter (54)

hydrolysis a chemical weathering process where minerals breakdown because of a reaction with ions such as H^+ from water (41)

─────────────── I ───────────────

ice wedging a mechanical weathering process that breaks apart rocks as water seeps into cracks, freezes, and then expands (39)

igneous rock a type of rock that is formed when molten rock cools and solidifies; it can be classified as being intrusive or extrusive depending on where it forms (24)

index fossil the preserved remains of an organism known to have lived during a specific time span; it is used to provide an estimate age of the rock layers where it is found (82)

inorganic matter material that was not once living (55)

intrusion magma that pierces, flows into, and solidifies in pre-existing rock formations (72)

intrusive rock a type of igneous rock that forms beneath Earth's surface as magma cools and solidifies (24)

island an area of land smaller than a continent and bound by water (53)

island arc a series of volcanic islands that results from the subduction of an oceanic plate beneath another oceanic plate (113)

isotope a different form of an atom determined by a change in the number of neutrons in its nucleus (74)

isthmus a narrow stretch of land that joins two larger land masses (53)

─────────────── K ───────────────

karst topography an area of land where the subsurface bedrock, often made of limestone or marble, is partially dissolved by water (48)

─────────────── L ───────────────

landslide the downward movement of rock, soil, mud, or various combinations of material (50)

Laurasia an ancient continent, originally the northern part of Pangaea, that broke up to become North America, Europe, and most of Asia (97)

lava molten rock that erupts at Earth's surface (18)

lava plateau an extrusive igneous rock structure that forms as low viscosity basaltic lava spreads out, cools, and solidifies building upon each layer over time (116)

Law of Original Horizontality sedimentary rock layers initially form in a horizontal layer, and any change from that position is due to the rock being disturbed later (69)

Law of Superposition in horizontal sedimentary rock layers, the older layers of rock are found below younger layers of rock (70)

liquefaction a phenomenon that occurs when the shaking motion of an earthquake causes water saturated sediment to act as a fluid (110)

lithification the process of converting loose sediment into solid sedimentary rock by compaction, cementation, and crystallization (25)

lithosphere the solid layer of rock that includes Earth's crust and uppermost mantle (98)

lithospheric plate a section of rigid lithosphere that moves over the asthenosphere, also known as a tectonic plate (98)

loam soil that has approximately equal proportions of fine and coarse grains (56)

Love wave a transverse seismic wave that travels along Earth's surface moving the ground from side-to-side (106)

luster the physical property of a mineral that describes the way light reflects off its surface (16)

---M---

mafic rocks and minerals that form from molten rock low in silicon dioxide molecules but rich in iron and magnesium (19, 98)

magma molten rock beneath Earth's surface (18)

magma chamber an accumulation of molten rock beneath Earth's surface (113)

magnitude a measure of an earthquake's relative size (108)

mantle the layer of Earth situated below the crust and above the core (98)

mass movement earth material transported down a slope by gravity (50, 109)

meander the bend or curve in a river as water flows along the path of least resistance (47)

mechanical weathering a process of physically breaking materials, such as rocks, into smaller pieces without altering the chemical composition of its components (39)

mesa an isolated hill of rock that forms as a result of a cap of hard rock that protects underlying layers from weathering and erosion. Further weathering and erosion will form a butte. (53)

mesosphere a region of the mantle below the asthenosphere which extends to the outer core (98)

metamorphic rock a type of rock that has undergone structural or chemical changes caused by an increase in heat, pressure, or by the replacement of elements by hot fluids (26)

metamorphism structural or chemical change to minerals within a rock caused by heat, pressure, or the replacement of elements by hot fluids (20)

microorganism a living organism that requires a microscope to see, such as bacteria (54)

mid-ocean ridge an underwater mountain range that forms where Earth's tectonic plates gradually move apart (100)

mineral a naturally occurring inorganic solid with a definite chemical composition; it can be identified by its physical and chemical properties and its crystal structure (14)

mineral replacement fossil the preserved remains of an organism where mineral-enriched solutions fill and crystallize the microscopic spaces within bones, shells, teeth, or woody plant tissue (80)

Modified Mercalli Intensity scale based on intensity readings I - XII, it measures the effect an earthquake has on the surface of Earth and on human built structures (109)

mold a hollow impression left by an organism that has decayed during the formation of sedimentary rock (80)

molecule a particle consisting of two or more chemically combined atoms (15)

molten rock a liquid mixture of dissolved pieces of rock, gases, and minerals (18)

moment-magnitude scale used to determine an earthquake's relative size (108)

moraine a general term used to describe sediment deposited by glaciers (52)

mudflow a water saturated mixture of rock debris and soil moving down a slope (50)

---N---

non-foliated metamorphic rock a rock formed from preexisting rock by pressure and/or heat that lacks a distinct banded or layered appearance (27)

normal fault a break in Earth's crust typically caused by diverging tectonic plates (104)

---O---

ore rock that contains useful minerals that can be mined and sold at a profit (21)

organic matter any material that was once living (54)

oxidation a chemical change that can occur when certain minerals are exposed to oxygen (41)

---P---

paleontology the study of the history of life on Earth as revealed through fossils (78)

Pangaea Greek for "all lands," the ancient supercontinent that included all the major landmasses on Earth (86, 97)

parent material the original substance from which rock, sediment, or soil is formed (39)

pegmatite a type of igneous rock that contains large mineral crystals (14, 18)

peninsula a mass of land connected by an isthmus and extending into a body of water (53)

period a unit of geologic time that divides eras and is subdivided into epochs (85)

physical property a characteristic of a substance that can be observed by its interaction with matter and energy without being changed chemically (16, 45)

plate tectonics the theory that Earth's lithosphere is broken up into plates which are slowly being moved over time by convection currents in the mantle (96, 101)

Precambrian Time the span of time that includes the Proterozoic, Archaean, and Hadean eons (84)

precipitation a chemical reaction in which solids form and separate from a solution (19)

preserved remains the tissue of once living organisms that has been protected from decomposition (81)

primary wave (P wave) a subsurface seismic wave that can travel through both the solid and liquid core of Earth moving particles in the same direction the wave travels (106)

Principle of Uniformitarianism concept that the geologic processes we see changing Earth's surface today have worked the same way in our geologic past (97)

pyramidal mountain peak the highest point of a mountain that forms a steep point caused by weathering and erosion (52)

pyroclastic flow the movement of volcanic debris, such as ash, pumice, rock fragments, and gas, down the side of a volcano that can reach speeds of more than 100 kph (62 mph) and temperatures greater than 500°C (932°F) (112)

---R---

radioactive decay the process where an unstable atom, over time, spontaneously releases energy breaking down to form a more stable atom (74)

radioactivity the natural release of energy by unstable atoms (74)

radiometric age the approximate age of a fossil, rock, or an event in geologic time calculated in years using radiometric dating techniques (76)

Rayleigh wave a surface wave, generated by seismic activity, that causes the ground to move in a circular motion (106)

relative dating placing layers of rock, fossils, or geologic events in chronological order so that ages can be compared (69)

reverse fault a break in Earth's crust that is typically caused by converging tectonic plates (104)

Richter scale developed by Dr. Charles Richter in 1935, it is used to determine an earthquake's relative size (108)

rift a linear zone of volcanic activity and faulting on Earth's crust caused by diverging tectonic plates and tension forces (100)

river mouth the section of a river where it enters a lake or the sea (52)

rock solids that can be made up of a combination of minerals, fragments of other rocks, or the remains of plants or animals (14, 24)

rock cycle a set of linked geologic processes that describes the transformations between igneous, metamorphic, and sedimentary rocks (30)

rock fall occurs when sediment of any size drops from a cliff (50)

runoff the overland flow of water from precipitation (47)

─────────── S ───────────

sandbar an off-shore ridge of sand-sized sediment built up by moving water and lying parallel to the coast (52)

sea cliff a steep coastal rock face formed by wave erosion (53)

sea-floor spreading the process by which new oceanic crust is formed at divergent boundaries (101)

seamount an underwater mountain usually formed by volcanic activity (102)

secondary wave (S wave) a sub surface seismic wave that moves particles perpendicular to the direction the wave travels (106)

sediment solid pieces of rocks, minerals, or remains of plants or animals that range in size and can be transported by erosion (25, 47)

sedimentary rock a type of rock that is formed from accumulated deposits of rocks, minerals, or the remains of plants or animals (25)

seismic wave a progressive disturbance that transfers energy from an earthquake in all directions both below and on Earth's surface (106)

seismic zone an area where earthquake activity occurs frequently and consistently (104)

seismograph an instrument that detects, records, and measures the intensity, duration, and direction of seismic waves (107)

seismology the study of earthquakes (107)

shear force occurs when two sides of rock layers slide past one another in opposite directions creating shear folds and strike-slip faults (105)

shield volcano a large extrusive rock formation with a broad base and gentle slope (116)

silicate a common group of minerals that contain silicon and oxygen molecules (19)

sill an igneous intrusion that squeezes between layers of pre-existing rock (117)

slump the down slope movement of an intact mass of rock and soil (50)

soil loose mixture of weathered rock particles, organic matter, mineral fragments, water, and air (54)

soil horizon a layer of soil that is different in color, texture, and composition to the layers above and below it (57)

soil profile the combination of horizon layers within the soil (57)

solution a homogenous mixture of more than one substance (19)

stalactite a mineral deposit shaped like an icicle that hangs downwards from a roof or wall of a cave (20)

stalagmite a mineral deposit, usually cone-shaped, rising upwards from a cave floor (20)

stratigraphy the study of rock layers (69)

streak the color a mineral leaves behind when it is rubbed against a hard surface or broken down into a powder (16)

strike-slip fault a break in Earth's crust typically caused by plates sliding horizontally to one another (104)

subduction a geologic process where a tectonic plate sinks below a less dense tectonic plate as the two plates collide (105)

surface area measure of area on the outside of an object (45)

surface waves the slowest seismic waves produced by an earthquake, which includes Love and Rayleigh waves (106)

syncline downward folding of layers of rock that look similar to a bowl-like concave upwards shape (71)

─────────── T ───────────

tectonic plate a section of rigid lithosphere that moves over the asthenosphere, also known as a lithospheric plate (98)

tension force occurs at divergent plate boundaries where rock layers pull apart and stretch causing thinning of rock layers and the formation of normal faults (105)

trace fossil the preserved remains of an animal's activity (81)

transform boundary the region where tectonic plates slide horizontally past each other (102)

transverse wave a type of mechanical wave in which the wave energy causes matter in the medium to move up and down or back and forth at right angles to the direction the wave travels (106)

trench deep sections of the ocean floor created by the subduction of a tectonic plate (105)

tsunami a sea wave produced when water is displaced by events such as earthquakes, landslides, or volcanic eruptions (109)

─────────── U ───────────

unconformity the area where the processes of weathering, erosion, deposition, and lithification have caused a gap in the geologic record (71)

─────────── V ───────────

valley an elongated depression on the surface of the land usually carved out or shaped by water erosion from rivers, streams, or glaciers (52)

vent an opening in Earth's crust where magma is forced up and flows out as lava (101)

viscosity a liquid's resistance to flow; a highly viscous fluid does not flow easily whereas a less viscous does (112)

volcanic island a land mass that forms from the ocean floor as layers of extrusive igneous rock build up and pierce the ocean's surface (113)

volcanic neck the solidified magma in the pipe-like channels of a volcano that becomes exposed as overlying layers of sedimentary rock are weathered and eroded away (117)

volcano an opening in Earth's crust where hot molten rock, ashes, gases, and/or rock fragments erupt (38, 112)

─────────── W ───────────

weathering chemical and mechanical processes at or near Earth's surface that break down materials, such as rocks and minerals (38)

Credits

The JASON Project would like to acknowledge the many people who have made valuable contributions in the development of the *Operation: Tectonic Fury* curriculum.